CW00538102

Murder or ~~~~~

Thomas Slemen is a freelance journalist who has written articles and features for the *Financial Times*, the *Liverpool Echo*, the *Daily Post* and many magazines in Britain, France and the United States. He is interested in Fortean phenomena and local mysteries, and recently produced a tourist guide to the off-beat side of his home town called *Strange Liverpool*.

Murder on Merseyside

THOMAS SLEMEN

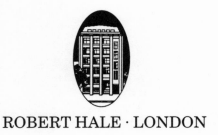

ROBERT HALE · LONDON

© *Thomas Slemen 1994*
First published in Great Britain 1994

ISBN 0 7090 5579 X

Robert Hale Limited
Clerkenwell House
Clerkenwell Green
London EC1R 0HT

The right of Thomas Slemen to be identified as
author of this work has been asserted by him
in accordance with the Copyright, Designs and
Patents Act 1988.

Photoset in North Wales by
Derek Doyle & Associates, Mold, Clwyd.
Printed in Great Britain by
St Edmundsbury Press Ltd, Bury St Edmunds, Suffolk.
Bound by WBC Ltd, Bridgend, Mid-Glamorgan.

Contents

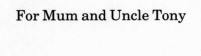

For Mum and Uncle Tony

Acknowledgements

The author wishes to thank the staff at Liverpool Central Library and Sydney Jones Library for use of their microfilm and microfiche machines. I would also like to thank Chief Superintendent Ken Hoskisson of Merseyside Police for his assistance and advice.

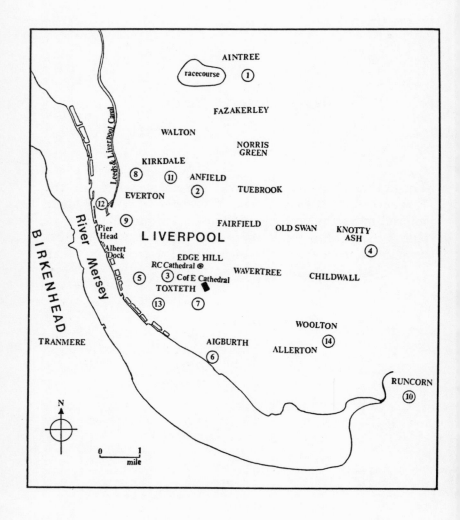

AINTREE

racecourse ①

FAZAKERLEY

WALTON

NORRIS
GREEN

KIRKDALE

⑧   ⑪   ANFIELD

EVERTON   ②   TUEBROOK

⑫

⑨

Pier
Head   FAIRFIELD   OLD SWAN   KNOTTY
ASH

LIVERPOOL

④

Albert
Dock   EDGE HILL
RC Cathedral ⊛

⑤   ③ C of E Cathedral   WAVERTREE   CHILDWALL

TOXTETH

⑬   ⑦

WOOLTON

⑭

TRANMERE   AIGBURTH   ALLERTON

⑥

RUNCORN

⑩

River Mersey

BIRKENHEAD

Leeds & Liverpool Canal

N

0   1
mile

Foreword

Like every other English county, Merseyside has had its fair share of murders over the years. This casebook contains various accounts of individuals who broke the sixth Mosaic commandment – 'Thou shalt not kill' – and it also contains cases where it is difficult to establish if an act of murder was actually committed at all. Take the intriguing case of the Man in the Iron Tube, which refers to a Victorian cadaver found in a sealed metal cylinder. How the nineteenth-century man came to be a canned corpse is still a mystery, as is the cause of his death. The murders detailed in this book span 178 years, from John Bellingham's assassination of the prime minister in 1812 to the case of the Pyre in the Alley, which occurred in 1990.

It is sad to relate how violent crime on Merseyside and in the rest of the world has evolved since the days of Bellingham's crime, when Britain did not have a police force at all. In January 1992 Merseyside police introduced Armed Response Vehicles (known as ARVs) into the region to tackle the alarming number of hold-ups and other firearms-related crimes that seem to be proliferating in the cities of Britain. Nineteen national forces now use ARVs, which are armed with Heckler Koch carbines, the weapons the SAS used to storm the

Iranian Embassy in London in 1980. The German-made firearm is highly accurate, self-loading, and fires 9mm handgun bullets. It is also equipped with a powerful Mag Lite torch for illuminating night-time targets. The Smith & Wesson Model 10.38 calibre revolver is also carried in the ARVs, and many other guns are becoming available to specialist police officers. In an interview with the *Liverpool Echo* in April 1994, Merseyside chief constable James Sharples gave a chilling warning to armed thugs. He told them, 'If you live by the gun, be prepared to die by the gun ... if there's a threat to the police or public we will shoot.'

In the year Mr Sharples made his remark, Merseyside police had made a record number of gun seizures, which included a cache of automatic weapons found in a flat in the Fazakerley district, eighty Italian shotguns found in a Bootle house, four machine guns buried in Formby and thirteen machine guns discovered at a flat in Everton.

Thomas Slemen
Liverpool, 1994

1 The Old Curiosity Shop Murder

In most people's minds the Liverpool district of Aintree is usually associated with its racecourse, where the world-famous Grand National is run each year, but early in 1953 Aintree featured in the newspaper headlines because a timid old man was brutally murdered within its vicinity.

Just a mile from Aintree racecourse, there stands a grand Victorian detached house, 98 Warbreck Moor. It was once the home of George Walker, a retired and increasingly reclusive 82-year-old tailor who liked to hoard antiques and bric-a-brac in the shop he ran on the ground floor of his house. This magpie's nest was known to the locals as the 'Old Curiosity Shop', and at 2.30 p.m. on Friday 9 January 1953 twenty-year-old John Todd called to Walker's premises. Todd, a pale-faced man with a prominent pointed nose and a distinctive wart at the side of his right eye, loved to tinker about with anything mechanical, and broken watches and clocks were his speciality.

Old Mr Walker's sister, Mary, who lived in the Tuebrook district of Liverpool, immediately thought there was something sinister about the pallid young man. As he entered the shop, she noticed a knife dangling in a sheath attached to Todd's waistband. Mr Walker apparently liked Todd, and let him work unsupervised among his stock upstairs. Mr Walker told his sister that Todd was working on a troublesome grandfather clock.

Mary Walker saw Todd again on Monday the 12th. He was still attempting to fix the grandfather clock, and now seemed very familiar with her brother, calling him 'Pop' and joking with him.

On the afternoon of 13 January two schoolboys – Ronald Cole and Allan Lake – called at Walker's shop, hoping to purchase valves for a radio set, but John Todd answered the door and told them to come back the next day.

On the following day at around 2.15 p.m., John Todd picked up the axe that Mr Walker used to break up large lumps of coal for his fire. He brought it down on the head of the 82-year-old man a total of thirty-two times. After a couple of blows, Mr Walker's legs gave way and he collapsed on to the vestibule floor at the foot of the staircase. As Walker lay there, spreadeagled, the savage John Todd continued to whack the old man's head. Pieces of skull flew across the hallway during the sickening assault, and bloody brain-tissue spattered the walls – and Todd's fawn-coloured raincoat. Fifteen seconds into the attack, the axe's shaft broke, preventing the clock-mender from continuing his merciless slaughter.

John Todd saw what he had done. The well-liked, introverted old man rested in an ever-widening pool of blood. The silver pocket-watch, once of enormous sentimental value to its owner, was snatched from Walker's waistcoat. Todd walked upstairs to the scullery in a daze and dropped the blood-coated axehead in an enamel bowl of water. He discarded the stained raincoat, then returned to the hallway and walked through the pool of warm blood on his way to the front door of number 98. His crepe soles squelched as he went. Todd left the shop with the silver pocket-watch that he had murdered for.

Out in the street Mr Walker's two dogs – an old Scottish

terrier and a young mongrel – started to whine, as if they had some sense of their owner's violent demise. They ran to the door of the shop and began to bark, but passers-by thought there was nothing sinister about the behaviour of the distressed animals.

At 7.40 p.m. John Todd visited his 22-year-old girlfriend at her home of 2 Park Grove, in the Bootle district of the city. Raven-haired Iris Tucker had met John Todd eighteen months earlier while working as an usherette at the Bedford Cinema in the Walton district, and it had been love at first sight. Since that night when their eyes met, Todd had visited her every night, although Iris's father wasn't keen on her boyfriend, and hardly spoke to him.

Iris noticed that Todd was not wearing his sheath knife, and asked him what had become of it.

'I won't be wearing it anymore, love,' was Todd's enigmatic reply.

Back at Warbreck Moor, Mr Walker's dogs were still barking, and they continued to bay into the night. The commotion woke a neighbour of Mr Walker, and she went to the shop and rang the bell. Mrs Lawson knew how long it took for the decrepit shop-owner to answer the door, so she waited – and waited. Twenty minutes later she stopped hammering on the shop door, and decided to return home. She surmised that Mr Walker had gone to visit his sister.

Almost twenty-four hours later, the exhausted dogs were still whining at the door of Walker's shop. The mongrel suddenly parted company with the Scottish terrier and ran off to the next street. It went to the door of Mrs Owen, a woman who often treated Walker's dogs to the occasional bone. The mongrel barked at Mrs Owen's front door, and when she answered and saw the fretful animal, she knew something was wrong. After getting no answer at the Curiosity Shop, Mrs Owen phoned the police and told them that she had reason to believe that something dreadful had happened to old Mr Walker.

Sergeant Hosker of Rice Lane Police Station quickly responded to the call. He hammered on the door of number 98, and after receiving no reply, charged at the door and forced it open. Hosker took a small torch from his pocket and shone it into the dark hallway. The disc of light flitted about the walls of the corridor, then stopped on the body of George Walker. The sergeant found the lightswitch and flicked it, and a dim lightbulb revealed the heinous scene – but the sergeant was unaware of the faint trail of bloody footprints left by John Todd's shoes. Hosker shook his head as he surveyed the slivers of skull scattered about the hallway. The policeman had seen some stomach-turning sights in his time, but he had never seen a murder victim of Mr Walker's advanced age, and this really sickened him.

Fearful of disturbing evidence, Hosker retreated from the murder house and looked sympathetically at Mr Walker's dogs, who tilted their heads quizzically as they looked on at their dead owner. Sergeant Hosker closed the door and went to his car to radio the news of his gruesome discovery.

Chief superintendent Herbert Balmer headed the inquiry and his first action was to call for the services of the brilliant Home Office pathologist, Dr Arthur St Hill of the Huyton area of Liverpool. He promptly arrived at the murder scene and had the body of George Walker taken to the city mortuary, where a thorough post-mortem was carried out. Dr St Hill told Balmer of the thirty-two lacerations on the deceased man's skull and face. The skull and left cheekbones had been smashed during the prolonged attack, and Dr St Hill had managed to fit some of the bone fragments together like a grotesque jigsaw puzzle.

Balmer immediately arranged for the area surrounding

the 'Old Curiosity Shop' to be cordoned off, and a house-to-house inquiry disrupted the sleep of almost a hundred residents in the streets around Warbreck Moor. Later, around 6 a.m., Dr J.B. Firth and a gaggle of forensic experts invaded Walker's shop. They examined the crimson streaks on the walls of the hallway, and they also came to notice the faint outline of the bloody footprints. The forensic team employed the recently discovered technique of photographing the footprints in special lights that had been designed to enhance faint outlines by illuminating them from an oblique angle. In the developed photographs the footprints of John Todd showed up clearly.

The broken axe handle near the body fitted exactly with the piece of broken shaft that was still connected to the axehead in the bowl of water upstairs. What was obviously the murder weapon was taken away for analysis.

Two days later Balmer attended a press conference and revealed that the police were seeking a man of about thirty who mended clocks and watches for a living. Balmer gave the description of this sought-after individual: 'He has a thin pale face, a long pointed nose, and a distinctive whitish wart at the side of his left eye. He is about 5 feet 8 inches tall, and was last seen wearing a fawn-coloured gaberdine raincoat.'

Balmer and his detectives had heard a variety of descriptions of Todd during their enquiries, but the descriptions given by Mary Walker and the two schoolboys who had visited the shop on the day before the murder had been invaluable.

Almost a week after the murder Todd's girlfriend, Iris Tucker picked up the morning paper and read of 'The Old Curiosity Shop Murder'. She sipped a cup of tea as she perused the newspaper's account of the terrible deed, and was sickened by the article. She wondered how anybody could stoop to killing a defenceless old man. Iris's heart skipped a beat when she read of the man wanted by the police. In total disbelief she read and re-read of the watch-mender with the wart at the side of his left eye. Iris shared her fears with her father, who told her that they had no choice but to inform the police. He grabbed his coat and walked to the nearest telephone box to call Bootle Police Station. Detective Chief Inspector Morris, Detective Sergeant Metcalfe and Detective Constable Hall arrived at 2 Park Grove and quizzed Iris Tucker. She told the policemen what they wanted to know, and within fifteen minutes they were knocking on the door of a house in Roxburgh Street, Walton, where John Todd lived with his mother. Todd was taken to Rice Lane Police Station and grilled for almost five hours before being charged with the murder of George Walker.

'No,' was Todd's reaction to the charge. His voice was barely audible.

'Eh?' Chief Inspector Morris said to him.

'Only I know I didn't murder him.' Todd replied.

On the following day, as George Walker was being buried in Everton Cemetery, John Lawrence Todd found himself in court before Liverpool stipendiary magistrate Arthur McFarland. The accused was represented by Harry Livermore, and the prosecuting solicitor was Mr A.E. West. West told the court of Todd's far-fetched version of the events that occurred in the shop on the day of the murder. In his signed statement Todd said:

As I was leaving on the Wednesday, the old man tripped and fell against me. His nose hit my shoulder and started bleeding. His nose rubbed down the front of my raincoat as I tried to get my hands under his arms to try to stop him falling down, but I did not succeed. I then helped him up to see what had caused him to trip. I saw a type of adze or axe on the floor. I picked up the head, as the handle was broken, took the head up to the kitchenette and put it on the bottom shelf of the food cabinet.

Things were looking very grim for the accused, and at the end of the three-day hearing, Todd was committed for trial at Liverpool Assizes at St George's Hall on 8 April 1953.

At the start of the trial, Todd pleaded not guilty to the charge of murder. Prosecuting counsel Edward Wooll QC informed the jury – which consisted of ten men and two women – of the claims made in Todd's statement, then called for Dr J.B. Firth, the forensic expert, to provide his evidence. Firth told the court of the blood found inside the trouser pocket and jacket cuff of Todd's blue suit. George Walker's blood was Group O. The blood on Todd's suit was also Group O. This same type of blood was detected on Todd's fawn raincoat – found at the scene of the crime. Blood of Group O was also found on the uppers of Todd's pair of brown crepe-soled shoes, although Firth stated that he had found no blood on the soles.

Dr Arthur St Hill was called to give evidence, and he presented the court with the findings of the post-mortem carried out on the murdered man. Dr St Hill also gave details of the bloody footprints discovered in the hallway of Mr Walker's shop, and he calmly gave a blow-by-blow account of a grisly experiment he had arranged during the course of his investigation. Several members of the jury looked queasy as Dr St Hill described how he had got a laboratory worker at the forensic unit in Preston to stand in a tray of human blood, wearing crepe soles to soak up the blood. Dr St Hill asked the lab worker to walk specific distances on the pavement outside the building in order to discover how long it would take for the blood to be walked off the soles. The macabre experiment was carried out on a rainy day, and Dr St Hill found, to his surprise, that there was no detectable blood on the crepe soles after the lab worker had walked 400 yards. Therefore the absence of blood on Todd's crepe shoes was no indication of his innocence.

Mr Wooll later called Todd's girlfriend to the witness box. Iris told the court how she had come to meet John Todd and how long she had known him. She was shown a pair of brown crepe-soled shoes, a fawn raincoat, and a blue suit. Wooll asked Iris Tucker if she had seen these items of clothing before, and Iris said that the exhibits had been worn by Todd on the day of the murder.

During evidence to the court, Iris said that her boyfriend had mentioned losing his raincoat on the day of the murder, while he claimed to be looking for work at Sandon Dock. Iris also told how – hours after the murder – Todd had called to her house wearing a blue suit unlike the blue suit he usually wore.

Mary Walker, the sister of the murdered man was called to the witness box, and she told the court about Todd's visits to the shop to fix the grandfather clock, and what she said was corroborated by Ronald Cole and Allan Lake – the schoolchildren who had spoken to Todd after calling at the shop on the day before the murder.

David Harrison, a jeweller who had repaired Mr Walker's watch in September 1951, was given the watch found in the possession of John Todd, and Harrison said it was George Walker's silver pocket-watch. Wooll asked Harrison if he was sure, and the jeweller said he was absolutely certain.

Miss Rose Heilbron QC had the daunting task of presenting a realistic defence. She rehashed the dubious tale of Mr Walker falling against Todd with a bleeding nose, but the story seemed more contrived each time the court heard it. Miss Heilbron ended her examination by putting a question to Todd. She asked him if he killed George Walker, and in an unusually raised voice Todd replied: 'I did not kill Mr Walker!'

At this point Mr Justice Cassels said, 'I think this is a convenient moment to adjourn until tomorrow.'

Mr Wooll cross-examined John Todd on the following day, and he got him to admit that his raincoat had not been misplaced at Sandon Dock at all; but Todd then went on to say that although he had lied about the raincoat, the silver watch which David Harrison had identified as Mr Walker's was in fact his own. Todd was asked to elaborate on this claim, and the young man said he had received the watch from a mysterious man named John Arthur at the Bedford Cinema, some eighteen months ago.

Mr Wooll took hold of a graphic black-and-white photograph that showed the battered corpse of George Walker lying in the hallway, and he held the print up to Todd. As the young man blinked and looked away from the photograph, Wooll said, 'When the old man fell after bruising his nose, did he fall like that?'

'No,' Todd said, in a subdued voice.

'How did the bloodstains get on your raincoat?' Wooll asked.

'He just – he just bled on me,' was Todd's reply.

'So I take it that this gory mess is subsequent to your leaving?' said Wooll, pointing to the photograph.

'Yes.' Todd looked down at his hands.

The young man stepped down from the witness box after giving evidence for a duration of two hours and fifteen minutes.

During the final address to the jury, Wooll recounted the significance of the silver watch and the fawn raincoat.

Miss Heilbron gave her summary of Todd's weak defence, and she ended by saying, 'Todd comes to you not as a man with petty convictions or grave convictions against him, but as a man of sterling character, and if ever a character could be weighed in the balance, I am sure you will take that into account. Todd is a very ordinary young man living with his mother.'

And in his summing-up to the jury Mr Justice Cassels said, 'No man is to be convicted on a charge such as this merely because he told lies, but you are not to leave out of your consideration the reflection as to why he told lies. If you are satisfied that this was the hand that struck those thirty-two savage blows on that defenceless old man's head, and thus battered the life out of him, you will return a verdict of guilty.'

The jury returned a verdict of guilty after one hour of deliberation. As the black cap was placed on the head of Mr Justice Cassels, John Todd's face remained expressionless. Mr Justice Cassels said, 'The sentence upon you is that you be taken from this place to a lawful prison, and from thence to a place of execution, there to suffer death by hanging, and that your body be buried within the precincts of the prison in which you were last confined before your execution, and may the Lord have mercy on your soul.'

Defence counsel Harry Livermore lost no time in lodging an appeal, and Miss Helbron also appealed against Todd's conviction at the Court of Criminal Appeal. But Mr Justice Croom-Johnson dismissed the case, saying there was 'nothing in it'.

Livermore sent a letter to David Maxwell Fyfe, the home secretary, urging for a medical inquiry into Todd's sanity. 'I am unable to comply with the request,' was the home secretary's written reply.

And so executioner Albert Pierrepoint and his assistant John Broadbent were summoned to Walton Prison to dispatch John Todd. The young man who robbed the life of a frail old man was hanged on the Tuesday morning of 19 May 1953. A week after the execution the RSPCA found a new home for Mr Walker's pets — the faithful dogs that had first alerted the residents of Warbreck Moor to the terrible murder of their master.

2   A Fatal Attraction

Earlier this century a fine new church called the Temple of Humanity opened at 46 Upper Parliament Street, Liverpool. The religion or, rather, philosophy of those who attended the church was known as Positivism, a belief-system founded by Auguste Comte, the French philosopher and sociologist. The Positivists do not worship God, but are devoted to humanity and strive for the welfare of mankind. The Positivist creed was viewed by many as too abstract, and the adherents to the philosophy were, and still are, few and far between.

Today the Temple of Humanity is still standing, but is now known as the Third Church of Christ, Scientist. This building was the innocent focus of a series of dreadful deeds perpetrated one autumn evening in 1913. It all began some years before, when Mr Sydney Style, a solicitor, and the leader of the Positivists, was introduced to a handsome young Evertonian named William MacDonald. A carpenter and an ardent Marxist, MacDonald was highly interested in joining the Positivists, as he found their creed dovetailed with his communist beliefs. So MacDonald attended one of the *soirées* that were held every Thursday evening at 69 Hope Street, the home of Sydney Style and his wife. At these weekly evening parties MacDonald became

acquainted with other Positivists and spent many an
hour passionately discussing his views on socialism and
extolling dialectical materialism. But MacDonald had
another passion, and it was one he never dared to
express: she was 42-year-old Mary Crompton, the
daughter of the shipping magnate Albert Crompton, co-
founder of the Liverpool Positivists. Mary's grandfather,
Sir Charles Crompton was a justice of the Queen's Bench.

Mary was a very kind and understanding individual and
always found time to help people. She was well educated
and fluent in many languages. But the one thing she
seemed to lack in her life was a man, although she was quite
attractive and was desired by many of the red-blooded
males in the sect. One infatuated admirer was 24-year-old
Paul Gaze, an orphan who had been adopted by Miss
Crompton. On many occasions during his teens and
adulthood, Gaze confronted his patroness with his passion
for her, but she always rejected it. The nature of the love she
gave was strictly platonic. Gaze eventually found employment with a chemical manufacturing firm, and during a
trip to Brazil as a representative of the company, he met
and became engaged to a beautiful young Brazilian girl. He
brought his fiancée home with him and married her. Miss
Crompton was relieved. At last Gaze had found someone
nearer his own age-group. Nevertheless Miss Crompton
and Gaze were still good friends.

But the green-eyed monster in William MacDonald
saw it all wrongly. MacDonald thought the object of his
secret love was becoming increasingly fond of Gaze, and
he could not allow that. All his Marxist ideals of common
ownership were applicable to the material world, but as
far as Miss Crompton's benevolence was concerned – he
wished that to be directed to him alone.

So on the night of Tuesday 7 October 1913, at 9.30, the
emotionally torn MacDonald armed himself with a
revolver and a weighted stick, and went to the house of

Richard Price Roberts, the Copper engraver who had introduced him to the Temple of Humanity. As far as the demented MacDonald was concerned, Roberts was another rival. He also had been getting a bit too familiar with Miss Crompton of late ...

MacDonald rang the doorbell and waited. A few moments later the door opened wide and Roberts came out. Almost instantly MacDonald brought the stick down on Roberts' head, drew the revolver and fired it at him twice. One of the bullets missed and the other passed right through the victim's nose.

MacDonald then ran away, leaving his former friend with a bloody face and a bruised head, but alive.

Ten minutes later in Grove Street, Edge Hill, Mac-Donald met his imagined arch-rival in love, Paul Gaze. Gaze invited his friend to his nearby lodgings at number 62, and MacDonald accompanied him to the house. At 10.15 p.m. the maidservant at Gaze's residence heard two loud noises that sounded like a cane being rapped on a door. She then heard the sound of heavy running footsteps in the hall. When she went to investigate she noticed the front door of the house was wide open. She closed it and moments later she walked into the parlour. To her horror she saw Gaze lying dead on the hearth rug with a bullet would in his temple.

By now MacDonald was banging on the knocker of 81 Bedford Street South, where his beloved Miss Crompton lived. A maid answered and MacDonald asked for Miss Crompton. But the maid told him that her mistress had just retired to her room. MacDonald was insistent: he wished to see Miss Crompton about a matter of the utmost urgency. The maid relented and showed MacDonald into the sitting-room. A few minutes later Miss Mary Crompton, the innocent victim of her own fatal attractiveness, came downstairs to meet MacDonald. She entered the sitting room. William MacDonald came face to face with the object of his unrequited love. He raised the revolver, pointed it at her head and fired, killing her instantly. Seconds after her body hit the floor, MacDonald placed the barrel of the revolver against his own head and pulled the trigger to end the tragedy. He died from his self-inflicted injuries three hours later in the Royal Infirmary.

After the double murder and suicide, the Positivists gradually disbanded, and in 1947 the statue that had been representative of the sect – a mother and child – was taken down from its arched recess high on the front wall of the former temple.

3 *The Wallace Conundrum*

William Herbert Wallace was born to lower-middle-class
parents in Keswick in the Lake District in 1878. His first
job was a draper's assistant, but he found the occupation
boring and felt the urge to travel. He visited India, then
China, but was not impressed by what he saw. After
contracting dysentery, he returned home, physically
shattered, to re-evaluate his life.

Around this time he became an avid reader of the
Meditations, a classic written by the ancient Stoic
philosopher Marcus Aurelius. Wallace strongly identified
with Stoicism, which advocates freedom from passions
and desires, and he adopted the Stoic creed. This, in a
nutshell, is: Don't expect too much out of life, but strive to
improve it by discipline and hard work.

Wallace later became a Liberal election agent in
Yorkshire, where he met a pretty, dark-haired woman
named Julia Thorp. Julia was well read and familiar
with the classics. She spoke French, could execute
exquisite sketches, and played the piano. At last Wallace
had a companion who could converse at his intellectual
level, and he married Julia in Harrogate in 1913.

The outbreak of World War I put paid to Wallace's
political agent's job and after trying a succession of
unsatisfying occupations, he found stable employment as

an insurance agent at a branch of the Prudential
Assurance Company in Liverpool's Dale Street.

The Wallaces soon settled into their new home at 29
Wolverton Street, a quite little cul-de-dac in Anfield. For
sixteen years Wallace held the same job without
promotion, and during this period the couple led a rather
humdrum lifestyle. They had no children, nor any real
friends, and lived on less than £4 a week.

When Julia was in her early fifties she became very
frail and relied on the help of a charwoman once a week.
Almost every week her husband played third-rate chess
at the Liverpool Central Chess Club, where he was a
member. While Wallace was on his way to the club on the
evening of Monday 19 January 1931, a man was making
a tuppence phone call to set in motion a train of events
that would lead to his wife's death and put the insurance
agent on trial for her murder.

The time was 7.15 p.m. A man in a red public
telephone box on the corner of Breck Road and Rochester
Road lifted the receiver and asked the operator to
connect him with Bank 3581, the telephone number of
Wallace's chess club in North John Street. There was a
technical hitch, so the operator recorded the number of
the caller's box – Anfield 1627. Moments later the same
man called back and again asked for Bank 3581.

'Operator,' said the caller, 'I have pressed button A but
have not had my correspondent yet.'

The caller was then put through to the chess club,
where waitress Gladys Harley answered the call.

'Yes?' said the waitress.

'Is that the Central Chess club?'

'Yes.'

'Is Mr Wallace there?'

The waitress looked around the room, which was
almost empty, and called to Samuel Beattie, who was
captain of the chess club.

'Mr Beattie, someone's on the phone for Mr Wallace.'

'Well, he's not here yet,' said Beattie, glancing up from his game of chess, 'but he's down to play a game, so he should be along later.'

As Beattie continued his game, the waitress interrupted him again, saying, 'Will you speak to this man?'

Beattie reluctantly left the game and took the receiver off the waitress.

'Samuel Beattie, club captain here. May I help you?'

'Is Mr Wallace there?'

'No, I'm afraid not.'

'But will he be there?'

'I can't say. He may or may not. If he is coming he'll be here shortly. I suggest you ring up later,' replied Beattie, slightly ruffled.

'Oh no, I can't,' said the caller, 'I'm too busy. I have my girl's twenty-first birthday on and I want to do something for her in the way of business. I want to see him particularly. Will you ask him to call round to my place tomorrow evening at seven-thirty?'

Beattie replied that he would if he saw Mr Wallace, and asked for the caller's name and address.

'The name is Qualtrough. R.M. Qualtrough.'

'And the address?' said Beattie, getting ready to scribble it down.

'Twenty-five, Menlove Gardens East.'

Later, at about 7.45 p.m., Wallace came into the chess club and Beattie informed him of the call from a Mr Qualtrough.

'Qualtrough? Who is Qualtrough?' Wallace asked blankly.

'Well, if you don't know who he is, I certainly don't,' said Beattie.

'Is he a member of the club?' said Wallace.

'No,' replied Beattie. 'We've no one called Qualtrough.'

'I've never heard of the chap,' said Wallace, puzzled.

'What did he want?'

In response to this question, Beattie handed Wallace the piece of paper on which he had written down Qualtrough's address and the time of the requested meeting.

'Where is Menlove Gardens East?' said Wallace, reading the address.

Beattie didn't know, but went to ask a colleague. A few moments later he returned shaking his head. 'No, he's not much help, I'm afraid,' said Beattie.

'I've got a tongue in my head. I'll find it,' said Wallace, and he pulled out his notebook and scribbled down Qualtrough's details. The prospect of earning 20 per cent commission on an annuity for Qualtrough's daughter was irresistible to Wallace.

At ten o'clock on the following morning Wallace left Wolverton Street and rode a tram to Clubmoor where he began his rounds, collecting a few shillings here, paying out benefit there. It was quite an uneventful day.

His last call was at Eastman Road, where a woman wanted to know how she could surrender her policy. After explaining the procedure, Wallace returned to Wolverton Street at around 6.05 p.m. and had tea with Julia. Wallace then gathered several forms needed for the business transaction with Qualtrough and went upstairs to the bathroom. He washed his hands and face, then went into the bedroom where he changed his collar and brushed his receded hair.

At 6.45 p.m. Wallace patted Julia on the back and promised her he would be back as soon as possible. As he left the house via the back door, he told Julia to bolt the door after him. That, he would insist later, was the last time he saw his wife alive.

Twenty minutes later, at 7.06 p.m., Wallace boarded a number 4 tram at the junction of Lodge Lane and

Smithdown Road. He asked the conductor if the number 4 went to Menlove Gardens East. The conductor shook his head and told Wallace to get a tram numbered 5, 5a, 5W or 7.

Wallace went to get off the tramcar, but the conductor stopped him, saying: 'Stay on the car. I'll give you a penny ticket for a transfer at Penny Lane.'

Wallace thanked him and settled down in a corner seat in the tram's saloon. Four times during the journey Wallace reminded the conductor of his intended destination. At Penny Lane Wallace boarded a number 7 tram. When the tram reached the top of Menlove Avenue, the conductor, Arthur Thompson, called Wallace to the platform and pointed to a road running off Menlove Avenue.

'That's Menlove Gardens West,' said Thompson. 'You'll probably find the street you want in that direction.'

Wallace thanked the conductor and, stepping off the tram, explained, 'I'm a complete stranger around here.'

As Wallace strolled down Menlove Gardens West, he saw a woman coming out of a house. He quickly crossed the road and asked her about the location of Menlove Gardens East, but the woman said she had never heard of the place. Wallace, continuing on his quest for Qualtrough's home, next asked a young man in Dudlow Lane if he had heard of the elusive address. The young man had not. Wallace wondered if Beattie had misheard Qualtrough on the phone, so he decided to call at number 25 Menlove Gardens *West*. He rang the bell at that address and an old white-haired woman named Katie Mather came to the door.

'Does Mr Qualtrough live here?' Wallace asked, tensely.

'There's no one of that name here,' replied Mrs Mather.

'I'm looking for Menlove Gardens East, but they tell me there isn't any,' said Wallace, anxious to hear the old lady's reply.

'I don't know the name,' said Mrs Mather, and she told

Wallace that there were Menlove Gardens North, South and West only.

Wallace thanked the old woman for the information and bid her good night. Shortly afterwards, at 7.45 p.m., Wallace spotted PC James Sargent near Allerton Road. The insurance agent approached him and asked the policeman where Menlove Gardens East was. The policeman knew the district well and said there was no such place. Wallace thanked the policeman and started to walk away – then stopped and turned around: 'Is there anywhere that I could see a directory?'

PC Sargent told him to try either the post office or the police station.

Wallace suddenly looked at his watch and said, 'Will the post office still be open? Yes, it's not eight o'clock yet, is it? No, it's just a quarter to.'

The policeman pulled out his watch and glanced at it. 'That's right, it's just a quarter to.'

At the post office Wallace was told that no street directory was available, and the man behind the counter suggested he might see one at a nearby newsagent's. At the paper shop, Wallace reiterated his account of the search for what appeared to be a nonexistent address, and was handed a street directory. After examining the directory and finding no Menlove Gardens East, Wallace left the shop shortly after 8 p.m. and caught a tram home. On the trip back to Wolverton Street, Wallace felt uneasy about his fruitless odyssey, and remembered that there had recently been several robberies in his neighbourhood. He thought about Julia alone in the house.

At 8.45 p.m. John and Florence Johnston of 31 Wolverton Street were about to leave their house through the back door, when they noticed their neighbour, Mr Wallace walking down the entry from the direction of Breck Road.

'Good evening, Mr Wallace,' said Mrs Johnston.

In an anxious tone, Wallace said, 'Have you heard anything unusual tonight?'

'No, why?' said Mrs Johnston curiously. 'What's happened?'

Wallace explained that he had been away from home since 6.45 p.m. and that he had just discovered that the front and back doors of his home were locked on the inside. John Johnston told Wallace to try the back door again. If he found it still locked, Mr Johnston said he would try and gain entry with his own back door key.

Wallace returned to the back door and this time the handle turned without difficulty and the door opened. 'It opens now,' he mumbled and disappeared into the house, leaving the door ajar. The Johnstons remained outside, waiting. They heard Wallace calling for his wife, then about three minutes later their neighbour ran out of the house and into the yard.

'Come and see! She has been killed!' cried Wallace excitedly.

He led the Johnstons into the house. Close to the fireplace in the parlour lay the huddled corpse of Julia Wallace. Her head had been smashed into a bloody pulp, and parts of her brain had spilled out of her skull. Her left arm was outstretched towards the piano, and her eyes stared lifelessly at the pedals.

Wallace stood trance-like in the middle of the room, looking down at Julia's corpse. He suddenly stooped down and felt her left wrist for a pulse. There was none but the body was still warm.

'I'm going for the police. Don't disturb anything,' said Mr Johnston.

'Get the police and a doctor. But I don't think it's much use. They've finished her,' said Wallace.

As Mr Johnston hurried out of the parlour, Wallace and Mrs Johnston followed him, but turned off from the hall into the kitchen, where Wallace discovered that £4 was missing from a cashbox. Mrs Johnston picked up a number of coins which lay nearby. Upstairs Wallace found that a roll of pound notes left in an ornamental jar had not been touched by the intruder. He descended the stairs and went into the parlour again with Mrs Johnston. Tearfully surveying Julia's battered body, he said, 'They've finished her. Look at the brains.'

Mrs Johnston shuddered at his words.

Wallace walked around the body scrutinizing it. He stopped and suddenly drew attention to something previously unnoticed by himself and the Johnstons. 'Why, whatever was she doing with my mackintosh?'

The garment in question was tucked under Julia Wallace's right shoulder.

At 9.15 p.m. PC Fred Williams arrived at the scene of the murder by bicycle. He propped his cycle against the low front wall of number 29 and knocked on the door. A few moments later Mrs Johnston came to the front door but found the temperamental lock too much of a challenge. Mr Wallace came to her help, and somehow opened the door effortlessly. Wallace ushered the policeman in, saying, 'Come inside officer. Something terrible has happened.'

PC Williams entered the parlour and knelt by the body. After finding no pulse, the policeman listened to Wallace's story about the wasted journey to Menlove Gardens, then went on a tour of the house. Not long afterwards more police invaded the house. Hot on PC Williams's heels came Sergeant Breslin, then Whitley MacFall, a prominent professor of forensic medicine from Liverpool University who had been summoned to examine the corpse. He was followed by Detective Inspector Gold, Detective Sergeant Bailey and a police photographer and fingerprint expert. Then at 10 p.m.

Chief Superintendent Hubert Moor, the head of Liverpool CID, arrived with another police sergeant.

Moore, a red-haired Irishman, took a quick look at the body in the parlour and spoke to PC Williams. He then asked Wallace if either he or any of his neighbours had seen anyone loitering around the house before the murder. Wallace said that neither he nor his neighbours had seen anything suspicious. Moore then left the house and drove to the bridewell in Anfield Road to telephone all the details of the murder to an inspector at police headquarters in Dale Street. The inspector then alerted all the police divisions of the city, instructing them to be on the look-out for a heavily bloodstained man.

At about 10.30 p.m. Superintendent Moore returned to Wolverton Street and asked several detectives who were also arriving at the house to search for the murder weapon. Moore examined the recalcitrant but intact lock on the front door, and deduced that no one had broken in. He walked down the hall and turned into the kitchen to quiz Wallace again. As Wallace described his search for Qualtrough, Moore's eyes scanned the insurance man's clothing for any traces of blood. There was none. Moore then reached for the cashbox and opened it. He looked at Wallace and said, 'I can't understand why a thief would go to all this trouble putting the lid on the box and putting it back where he'd found it.'

Later that night Wallace found he could not make a proper statement in the crowded atmosphere of his home, so he was taken by police car to the Anfield Road bridewell where he could make some attempt to collect his thoughts in a quieter environment. At the bridewell Wallace was exhaustively interviewed by Inspector Gold and Sergeant Bailey.

At 4 a.m. Superintendent Moore finally left Wallace's home and drove to the Anfield Road bridewell. When Wallace saw Moore arrive, he asked him if there had been any developments in the case, but the superintendent had nothing further to report. Wallace then asked if he could go home to bed. Moore said that was not possible, but allowed Wallace to stay with his sister, Amy Wallace, at her flat in Ullet Road.

On Monday 2 February, at 7 p.m., a police car drew up outside 83 Ullet Road. Superintendent Moore, Superintendent Thomas and Inspector Gold got out of the car and walked up to the Amy Wallace's first-floor flat. A young man answered the door. It was William Wallace's nephew, Edwin. Moore asked Edwin if he could see his mother. Edwin said she was out, but admitted the three detectives into the flat. They accompanied Edwin to the sitting-room, where William Wallace was writing letters.

'Someone from the police station wants to see you, Uncle,' said Edwin to Wallace and simultaneously the detectives entered the sitting-room.

'Take a seat, gentlemen,' said Wallace. But the detectives didn't respond. They stood there without even removing their hats. Inspector Gold broke the silence.

'Mr Wallace, you know who I am?' he said.

Wallace nodded and was about to speak when Inspector Gold continued, 'It is my duty to arrest you on the charge of having wilfully murdered your wife, Julia Wallace, and I have to caution you that anything you may say in reply to the charge will be taken down in writing and used in evidence against you.'

'What can I say in answer to this charge, of which I am absolutely innocent?' said Wallace, stunned.

Nobody answered. The sound of Inspector Gold scribbling Wallace's reply in his notebook seemed amplified in the silence.

To his startled nephew, Wallace said, 'Edwin, they have come to take me away.'

'I'm awfully sorry, Uncle. Is there anything I can do?' said the boy in a broken voice.

The murder trial opened at the Liverpool Spring Assizes in St George's Hall, Lime Street, on Wednesday 22 April 1931. To the two prison officers standing on each side of the prisoner, the clerk of Assizes shouted, 'Put up Wallace!'

The officers immediately ushered Wallace up the steps and into the dock. Within a few tense moments there was a call for silence, and everyone in the court rose as the sheriff and his chaplain entered the room, followed by Mr Justice Wright in his goat's-hair wig. As the judge and clerks took their places, the pack of newspaper reporters up in the press box waited with their pencils and short-hand notebooks. The atmosphere was electric. The occasional cough and sniffle echoed from the crowd packed into the public gallery. Then the cold, official voice of the clerk of Assizes boomed, 'William Herbert Wallace, you are indicted and the charge against you is murder in that on the 20th day of January 1931 at Liverpool, you murdered Julia Wallace.'

Wallace looked down from the dock with a blank expression.

The clerk then asked: 'How say you, William Herbert Wallace, are you guilty or not guilty?'

In a resolute tone, Wallace replied, 'Not guilty.'

The jury was sworn in, and Edward George Hemmerde KC, began his opening speech for the Crown: 'Members of the jury, the prisoner at the Bar, William Herbert Wallace, is indicted, and the charge against him is murder, in that on the 20th day of 1931, at Liverpool, he murdered Julia Wallace. Upon his indictment he has been arraigned, upon his arraignment he has pleaded that he is not guilty and has put himself upon his country, which country you are, and it is for you to enquire whether he be guilty or not and to hearken to the evidence.'

For two hours the jury listened to Hemmerde's graphic account of the 'real' events leading up to the murder. Hemmerde promised the jury '… evidence which … will not show you any motive; nevertheless, what I shall suggest to you will carry you almost irresistibly to the conclusion that this woman was murdered by her husband.'

Hemmerde then began to throw doubt on the story of the Qualtrough phone call, saying, 'You may think it curious that a total stranger to the prisoner, speaking from a place 400 yards from his house … should have rung up the City Café [where the chess club met]; you would have thought that he might have called at the house; you would have thought that he might have written to the house; he might have left a note at the house!'

And of Wallace's expedition to Menlove Gardens the prosecutor suggested it was illogical for an experienced insurance agent to '… call the next night on someone he does not know, at an address which you will find does not exist'. To the jury Hemmerde said, 'Do you believe a tale like that?'

Mr Hemmerde then alerted the jury to the curious way in which Wallace had drawn attention to himself to support his alibi on his way to the fictitious Menlove Gardens East – speaking to the tram conductors and members of the public and, most blatant of all, discussing the exact time of the evening with a policeman.

As for Wallace's alleged difficulty in gaining access to his home after having returned to Wolverton Street, Hemmerde suggested, '… supposing you came to the conclusion that the doors never were shut against him … you then find a man who could perfectly well get in if he wanted to, pretending that he cannot get in'. The intimation was that Wallace had pretended he couldn't get into the house to ensure that he had witnesses not only to see him arrive home but also to observe his concerned demeanour and well-exhibited suspicion that all was not well.

Referring to the mackintosh found at the scene of the crime, Hemmerde suggested that it could have been used to protect the murderer from being splashed with blood. He told the court: 'The history of our criminal courts shows what elaborate precautions people can sometimes take. One of the most famous criminal trials was of a man who committed a crime when he was naked.'

Hemmerde was here referring to the Swiss valet Françoise Courvoisier, who cut the throat of Lord William Russell in 1840 while completely naked. Hemmerde continued: 'A man might perfectly well commit a crime wearing a raincoat as one might wear a dressing-gown ... with nothing on underneath – only naked flesh on which blood could fasten.'

Summarizing, Hemmerde added,

> This is not a case where you will be in any way concerned with other possible verdicts such as manslaughter. If this man did what he is charged with doing, it is murder foul and unpardonable. Few more brutal can ever have been committed ... this elderly, lonely woman literally hacked to death for apparently no reason at all. Without an apparent enemy in the world, she goes to her account, and if you think the case is fairly proved against this man, that he brutally and wantonly sent this unfortunate woman to her account, it will be your duty to call him to his account.

When the Crown counsel finally sat down, his version of events seemed unshakeable to the jury. Wallace had phoned the chess club, leaving a message for himself, and on the following night cold-bloodedly murdered his wife – perhaps, as Hemmerde had suggested, in the nude, or wearing only a mackintosh to prevent him being splashed with her blood.

Mr Roland Oliver rose to open for the defence. He cross-examined Samuel Beattie, who had conversed with Qualtrough by telephone on the eve of the murder.

'Do you know Mr Wallace's voice well?' said Oliver.

'Yes,' answered Beattie.

'Did it occur to you it was anything like his voice?'

'Certainly not,' Beattie replied.

'Does it occur to you now it was anything like his voice?'

'It would be a great stretch of the imagination for me to say it was anything like that,' said Beattie.

Oliver then produced a witness who swore he had spoken to Julia Wallace at 6.40 p.m. on the evening of the murder. The witness was Alan Close, the 14-year-old milk boy who regularly delivered to the Wallace household.

But despite Oliver's bold efforts the case against Wallace remained black, and on Saturday 25 April the trial reached its climax. The jury was out for only an hour. The verdict they returned was 'guilty'.

Like a true stoic, Wallace showed no emotion as the black cap was placed on the judge's wig.

'William Herbert Wallace,' said Justice Wright, 'the jury, after a careful hearing, have found you guilty of the murder of your wife. For the crime of murder, by the law of this country there is only one sentence, and that sentence I now pass upon you. It is that you be taken from hence to a place of lawful execution, and that you be there hanged by the neck until your be dead, and that your body be afterwards buried within the precincts of the prison in which you shall last have been confined. And may the Lord have mercy on your soul.'

Wallace was then led from the court to a waiting Black Maria which took him to Walton Gaol. He was stripped naked at the prison and was soon wearing a grey prison uniform. By now Wallace was no longer stoical. He was crying openly. He continued sobbing as the prison warders led him to the condemned cell. But Wallace appealed against the verdict, and the following month the unbelievable happened: his plea was upheld by the Court of Appeal. It was the first time in the history of British Law that the court had overturned a conviction for murder – on the grounds that the verdict had opposed the weight of the evidence. Wallace was freed.

He was reinstated in his old job, but many of his colleagues still had lingering doubts about his innocence, and backs were turned upon him. The whole affair haunted him so much that in the end he left his home in Anfield and retired to Meadowside Road in Bromborough. On 26 February 1933 Wallace died in Clatterbridge Hospital from renal cancer, aged fifty-four. He protested his innocence to the last.

For years the Wallace case was seen as the classic murder mystery and many great criminologists and crime writers, including Raymond Chandler, Edgar Lustgarten and Dorothy L. Sayers, have tried to solve it, but without success.

Then in 1980 Roger Wilkes, a new editor at Radio City, Liverpool's independent station, made an amazing breakthrough on the Wallace case. While researching the murder mystery for a radio feature called 'Who Killed Julia?' he actually managed to track down a strong suspect, whom Wallace himself had named to police during the murder investigation. This man was Gordon Parry, a shady character who had been twenty-two years old at the time of the murder. Wilkes discovered that Parry had driven a car into a garage on Moscow Drive on the night of the murder and asked a man named John Parkes to hose the vehicle down. Parkes said that Parry was in an agitated state. While Parkes was hosing down the car, Parry told him to wash the vehicle's interior as well. Parkes did this, and discovered a blood-soaked leather glove hanging out of a box. He became suspicious and realized that he was washing away evidence, but continued because he feared Parry, who was renowned for his violent temper.

Parkes said that Parry was in a local dramatic society and often phoned up people he didn't even know and talked to them in a disguised voice. Could he have been responsible for the Qualtrough message? Wilkes discovered that Parry had worked with William Wallace at the Prudential Assurance Company in 1928, and had even struck up an acquaintance with Julia Wallace.

But Wilkes was not really the first to finger Parry. Almost twenty years before Wilkes's investigation, one of Britain's leading crime experts, Joe H. Gaute told the occult and crime writer Colin Wilson that he was convinced the murderer of Julia Wallace was one Gordon Parry. Gaute came to this conclusion because of several facts he had gathered from a lengthy investigation of the case. Parry had a criminal record, and as a frequent visitor to the home of George Wallace, he would have known where the insurance agent kept the collection money. Also, at the time of the killing, Parry was heavily in debt.

After Wallace retired he lived in fear of Parry, as he was convinced that the young man was the killer of Julia. Indeed so frightened was the man from the Pru that he even installed an alarm button inside his front door as a safety measure. When the police questioned Parry about his whereabouts on the night of the murder, he told them that he had been out with his friends at the cinema. Although Parry's associates corroborated his claims, the police interrogated the young man so persistently that he later admitted his original account had been 'a mistake'.

With these facts in mind, Gaute decided to trace the whereabouts of Parry, and started looking him up in the London telephone directory. A Mr G. Parry was listed at a south London address. Gaute gave the address to crime writers Jonathan Goodman and Richard Whittington-Egan, and the two men visited Parry. A small but stout man with grey sleeked-back hair and a thin military moustache opened the door and smiled at the writers nervously, but didn't invite them in. Whittington-Egan and Goodman quizzed Parry on the doorstep. Although the murder suspect acted evasively in face of the grilling, he seemed to be familiar with every little fact about the Wallace case and appeared to know what had become of every person who had been involved in the murder investigation – as if he had read everything about the murder and was still following its aftermath.

Parry said little about William Wallace, but hinted tantalizing that the insurance agent was 'a very strange man ... sexually odd'.

Parry later moved to North Wales, where he died in April 1989, weeks before Roger Wilkes could question him for his ground-breaking radio feature.

4 Murder in the Fog

The following murder case, which is still unsolved, is one of the most baffling incidents in criminal history. It contains enough red herrings and twists and turns to tax the mind of Sherlock Holmes himself.

On the day of the murder Liverpool was enveloped in a dense, freezing fog that had lingered over the city for days and seemed to be thickening by the hour. On the Wednesday morning of 20 December 1961, at eight o'clock, 33-year-old Brian Dutton took a cup of tea upstairs to his wife, who was in bed, then left his semi-detached home at 14 Thingwall Lane, Knotty Ash, and embarked on a long and hazardous journey to Widnes, where he worked as a research chemist for ICI. At home were his 27-year-old wife Maureen Ann Dutton and his two sons, David, aged two, and a 22-day-old baby who had not yet been christened.

Mrs Dutton wanted to take David to see the Christmas crib at Childwall Parish Church, and around 11 a.m., when her mother-in-law called to the house, Mrs Dutton asked her if she could babysit while she took her son to the church. Her mother-in-law said she would be able to look after the baby in the afternoon and left the house around midday. However, at 1.30 p.m. Mrs Dutton's mother-in-law phoned from her home in Broadgreen

Road to say that she would not be able to come after all because of the thick fog.

At 6.10 p.m. Mr Dutton arrived home and was surprised to see that the house was in darkness. In the living-room he found his wife dead on the floor. She had been stabbed to death. In a dazed state Mr Dutton called his neighbours in and quickly summoned a doctor.

In the morning room the family's lunch lay half eaten on the table and there was nothing to indicate that a struggle had taken place. Nothing had been stolen and there were no signs of a forced entry. For Mr Dutton the next traumatic experience, after discovering the body of his wife, was finding little David in the living-room. He was upset and he appeared to have witnessed the murder, although he and his baby brother had not been harmed.

The police were called and immediately launched an intensive roadcheck of all vehicles in the area, but it yielded nothing.

Chief Superintendent James Morris, head of Liverpool CID, led the investigation into what would subsequently be referred to in the newspapers as the 'Knotty Ash Murder', and Old Swan Police Station became the murder squad headquarters. After examining the murder scene, Morris mustered a hundred detectives with tracker dogs and co-ordinated a search of the Knotty Ash area. The frozen ground in the rear garden of the Duttons' home was raked in the search for the murder weapon, and a squad of Corporation workmen probed the drains of Thingwall Lane for the same reason. In a statement to the press Chief Superintendent Morris appealed to bus conductors on the nearby Thomas Lane route to contact the police if they had noticed anyone acting in a suspicious manner while boarding a bus between 1.30 and 6.30 p.m. on the day of the murder.

At noon the following day, Mr Herbert Balmer, the

deputy chief constable of Liverpool, visited the house
with several detectives, a photographer and a
fingerprint expert. During their examination of the
house, an auxiliary postman called to deliver several
Christmas cards. He too was asked if he had noticed
anyone suspicious in the area around the time of the
killing. He hadn't.

Meanwhile the only witness to the Knotty Ash Murder,
little David Dutton – who was now staying with his
younger brother at his grandmother's home at
Broadgreen Road – was being kept under constant
observation by a policewoman. Attempts had been made
to question the 2-year-old about the events he had
witnessed, but the child was largely incoherent. Still, the
policewoman listened to the child's babble for clues.

Chief Superintendent Morris racked his brains in
order to fathom possible motives for the fatal stabbing,
but could find none. The major questions remained
unanswered. Mrs Dutton had been stabbed fourteen
times in a frenzied attack by someone she had apparently
admitted into the house; did this mean the killer was
someone known to the murdered woman? Robbery was
evidently not the motive, for nothing had been stolen.
And why was there no sign of a struggle?

A basic reconstruction of the murder was put together
from the forensic examinations. It appeared that Mrs
Dutton had retreated from the front door with a knife
pressed against her throat. She had staggered backwards
across the hall and into the living-room, where she was
killed in front of her two children.

Morris gave a lot of thought to the victim-knew-the-
killer theory, and via another press statement he urged
everyone who had known the murdered woman since her
marriage in April 1958 to come forward.

In response to the police appeal to the bus conductors
on the Thomas Lane route, a piece of information

emerged that seemed to be the breakthrough Morris was hoping for. At 4.30 on the afternoon of the murder, a woman boarded the number 10d bus en route from Longview to the city centre in East Prescot Road, opposite Eaton Road. The woman was in an agitated state and out of breath, as if she had been running for quite a distance. In an Irish accent she said to herself that she had to get out of Liverpool immediately, and was going to London to catch a plane. She got off the bus at Lime Street and throughout the journey was heard muttering to herself repeatedly, 'Oh my God! Oh my God!' The woman was described as tall and buxom, and between twenty-five and thirty-five years old. She was wearing a pale pink coat, black shoes with stiletto heels and was carrying a white 'envelope' type of bag.

As Morris pondered the report of the Irish woman, the search for the murder weapon – thought to be a narrow-bladed knife – was getting into full swing. An inch-by-inch search of the area around Thingwall Lane produced nothing; the grounds of Thingwall Hall Mental Home were probed with mine detectors until dark; and in the nearby fields detectives working shoulder to shoulder used forks to examine the long grass. But all their efforts proved in vain.

Back at the murder house a detective discovered a light brown leather knife sheath. Mr Dutton said it did not belong to the family. The sheath appeared to be home-made and measured 5½ inches long and 1½ inches wide.

By this time another piece of information had come to light that offered a plausible motive for the killing of Maureen Dutton. On the day before the murder a woman, who, like Mrs Dutton, had recently given birth, was at her home in Halewood when a man professing to be a doctor called to examine her. The doctor's appearance and general demeanour gained the young woman's confidence; but when her husband later discovered that there was no doctor in the area with the name given by the man, he quickly informed the police. The bogus doctor was described as dark with a broad nose and cropped curly hair. He wore horn-rimmed spectacles and a dark grey overcoat, and was aged between twenty-seven and thirty.

Was he the cowardly fiend who had come out of the fog to call at the home of Maureen Dutton pretending to be a doctor wanting to examine her. Had Mrs Dutton been murdered by him after she had seen through his perverted disguise? Morris was considering the bogus doctor theory when the line of inquiry shifted once again. Several residents interviewed during the continuing house-to-house enquiries in the area claimed that a suspicious-looking young stranger in a leather jacket had been seen walking along Thingwall Lane towards Thomas Lane at about 1.50 p.m. on the day of the murder.

All Christmas leave for the policemen working on the Dutton case was cancelled. As the door-to-door enquiries continued, detectives heard more and more about the young man in the black leather jacket. Other interviews, however, were being conducted along another line. Morris and Balmer questioned many people who had visited the home of the dead woman over the past few years, and as a result of these interviews, the course of their investigations suddenly took a bizarre twist. Morris and Balmer apparently believed that members of a South Seas cult had been at the Dutton home in recent months and hypothesized that Mrs Dutton could have been the victim of a ritual murder.

Balmer and other detectives read up on the activities of the disciples of the Polynesian god Tiki, and discovered that worshippers made sacrifices to Tiki during the winter solstice – and Mrs Dutton had been murdered during this period. At the beginning of the 1960s the Polynesian cult had a considerable following in Britain and there were many members in Liverpool; so Balmer and several other detectives called at the homes of known members and at the many coffee bars and nightclubs throughout the city which the disciples were known to frequent. Detectives even visited record shops and listened to Polynesian music.

Once again the investigation appeared to have reached a dead end – until 4 January 1962, when a 24-year-old male nurse living in Upper Parliament Street was arrested and charged with the theft of drugs and surgical equipment from three Liverpool hospitals. He was also suspected of having masqueraded as a doctor. The police thought they had collared their man at last, especially since the male nurse had a tattoo on his right arm depicting a reversed swastika – the identification mark of a Tiki-worshipper.

But during the trial at Liverpool City Magistrates Court, Rex Makin (for the nurse) poured cold water on the police's hopes. He told the court that the only drugs his client had taken had been sleeping pills, mild sedatives and vitamin K tablets. He also added that the defendant was a man of good character who had never been in trouble before. The nurse had merely had the 'disadvantage of having a tattoo mark on his arm which had led the police to think he might be connected with the murder of Maureen Dutton'.

The male nurse was eliminated from the murder inquiry and the search for the bogus doctor resumed. The police were back at square one.

In the mean time, the search for the elusive murder weapon in the drains of Knotty Ash and Dovecot resulted in the recovery of about one hundred knives of all types, scissors and even an old bayonet, but the murder weapon was not among them.

By 17 January police had amassed 20,000 statements, and one mysterious figure kept resurfacing among all the data: the young man in the black leather jacket. Despite an intensive appeal in the newspapers, the much-sought youth never came forward to account for his whereabouts on that foggy afternoon. On 18 January the *Liverpool Echo* made a unique contribution to the police investigation by printing a colour identikit picture of the man in the leather jacket on the newspaper's front page. By the following day more than sixty people had come forward to tell the police that they thought they recognized the likeness. Many were mistaken of course; but some filled in several interesting details about the youth. One woman said she saw a youth in a shiny black jacket on the afternoon of the murder being violently sick at the Methodist Church near the corner of Court Hey Avenue and Greystone. All the time the youth was vomiting, he kept his hands in his pockets for some reason.

Another woman, who lived only a stone's throw from Thingwall Lane, gave a chilling account of how a youth in a leather jacket called at her house on the day of the Dutton murder a short time before 1.50 p.m. As the woman opened the door, she was confronted by a youth who looked identical to the one in the identikit picture issued by police. He just stood on the doorstep without speaking, with a half-smile on his face, tapping his left hand with his right. Before slamming the door on the stranger, the woman noticed that the youth's hands were well-kept and suntanned, and that he had long slender fingers.

The months rolled by without any more leads; in desperation the police even sought the aid of Interpol. But it was useless. The murderers of Maureen Ann Dutton could not be found. Gradually, the newspaper columns on the case got smaller and smaller and today the case remains a mere puzzler for students of crime.

Perhaps the Knotty Ash Murder resulted from a botched housebreaking attempt. Maybe the youth in the leather jacket was a housebreaker, visiting Knotty Ash under the ideal cover of the fog. The area was then a fairly affluent suburb and Thingwall Lane was a residential street populated by professional and retired people. It is quite plausible that the agitated blonde woman with the Irish accent who boarded the 10d bus that afternoon was the housebreaker's look-out. Perhaps she had panicked at seeing her partner-in-crime emerge from the house spattered in blood. Perhaps the youth knocked on the door of Maureen Dutton's home and expected no answer, and was taken by surprise when someone came to the door. But there is a problem here. Even if the intruder was confronted by a woman, why should he stab her to death instead of fleeing back into the fog? How could he have been certain that none of Mrs Dutton's family or friends was at the house that afternoon?

Another possibility is that the murderer had no specific motive for killing because he or she was insane. A very short walk away from the scene of the crime there was (and still is) a home for the mentally ill. Around the time of the murder this institution had only recently been established in a building that had once been the site of St Edward's Orphanage. When the changeover occurred it was a very low-key affair and many of the local residents were not aware that the old orphanage now housed mentally ill patients. A coalman who delivered to St Edward's around the time of the Dutton murder told me that the patients at the home were only restrained from wandering off into Thingwall Lane by a wooden fence a mere three feet high. Is it possible that a patient with a violent streak could have acquired a knife and slipped off the premises to kill at random? Would that explain the apparent lack of motive? Or does the answer lie in some other direction? I feel certain that someone in Liverpool knows what happened on that fogbound winter day all those years ago. Should that person be reading these words, I hope he or she will do the decent thing and break the long silence.

5   The Leveson Street Massacre

One spring morning in the year 1849, a 29-year-old
music teacher named Ann Hinrichson placed a notice in
the front parlour window of her home at 20 Leveson
Street. The notice read: 'Furnished Apartments to Let'.

Mrs Hinrichson's Danish mariner husband, John, was
at sea on his ship *Duncan*, and so she was left with the
formidable task of running the household and rearing
her two sons, 5-year-old Henry George and 3-year-
old John Alfred. What's more, Mrs Hinrichson was also
expecting a third child. The fourth person living at the
house was the maidservant Mary Parr, a conscientious
and indispensable young woman who helped to reduce
Mrs Hinrichson's burden. As well as being a servant,
Miss Parr was also a very trustworthy friend of Mrs
Hinrichson.

Leveson Street, which ran from Great George Street to
Suffolk Street, was a busy thoroughfare in the
nineteenth century, and no doubt there were hundreds of
passers-by who glanced at the card in the window at
number 20. But of all those individuals, only one called in
to inspect the vacant rooms, and he was a 26-year-old
Irishman from Limerick who went under the name of
John Gleeson Wilson.

Wilson was shown the front parlour and the back

bedroom, and, finding them to his liking, he immediately paid a week's rent in advance and moved in. The Irishman claimed to be a carpenter employed by the Dock Estate, and Mrs Hinrichson was pleased at having such an upright and hard-working young man as a lodger. What Mrs Hinrichson didn't know was that Wilson already had adequate lodgings in Porter Street, off Great Howard Street.

That night around ten o'clock, young Mr Wilson said goodnight to Mrs Hinrichson and went to bed.

On the following morning Wilson rose early, and by 7.30 he was in a nearby pub in Great George Street, having a glass of ale for his breakfast. At this public house, the first move that led to the wholesale slaughter of four innocent people took place. Wilson suddenly asked the pub's landlady if she could provide him with a wafer to seal the envelope containing an important letter.

'No, I'm sorry,' she said. 'But I've got a stick of sealing wax. Will that do?'

Wilson used the wax to fix down the flap of the envelope, then asked the landlady if she would be so kind as to write the address on the envelope, as he could not write. The proprietress was not exactly a skilled writer either, and called for her daughter. To the landlady's daughter, John Wilson dictated the address that was to go on the envelope: John Wilson, Esq., 20 Leveson Street, Liverpool.

Shortly after leaving the pub, Wilson called to a passing youth and asked him if he wanted to earn a few pennies by delivering a letter. The youth nodded enthusiastically, and in his charming Irish brogue, Wilson explained what he had to do. 'When I go into the house [in Leveson Street], I want you to wait a few minutes, then I want you to knock. Ask the person who comes to the door if John Wilson lives there, and say that you have a letter for him from his employer. Got that?'

The youth nodded. Five minutes after Wilson entered the house, the youth carried out his instructions. He approached the door of number 20 and knocked. A few moments passed, then Miss Parr answered the door.

'Does John Wilson live here?' enquired the youth, as instructed.

'Yes. Here he is,' said Miss Parr. Wilson came to the door, and, after borrowing money from Mrs Hinrichson to pay the errand boy, returned to his room with the letter.

At around 11 a.m. Mrs Hinrichson visited the greengrocer's in St James's Street and ordered potatoes. Next she called at a chandler's to purchase two jugs, which she asked to be delivered to her house. She then returned home.

Early that afternoon an errand boy arrived at Mrs Hinrichson's house with the potatoes. Wilson came to the door, took the vegetables off the boy, went into the house, then returned to the door with the empty basket. Almost half an hour passed before the chandler's delivery boy arrived at the house with the purchased jugs. He rang the doorbell, but nobody answered. He lifted the knocker and brought it down hard several times over, but still nobody came to the door. The youngster then peeped through the keyhole – and saw a pair of feet lying across the hall. This made the boy curious, so he climbed the railings in front of the parlour and looked in through the window. What he saw made his stomach turn. The parlour was like an abattoir. In scarlet pools lay the bodies of Mary Parr and little Henry. The errand boy almost fell from the railings with the shock. He jumped down and ran off, looking for a policeman. In Great George Street, the terror-stricken youngster ran straight into the arms of a policeman.

'What's to do, lad?' said the policeman, trying to calm the terrified boy down.

'Murder!' cried the boy, all out of breath.

'Eh? Now then, son. That isn't funny,' the policeman retorted angrily.

But the boy assured the policeman that he wasn't making it up and urged him to come to the house in Leveson Street to see for himself.

Meanwhile a young girl who was a pupil of Mrs Hinrichson was arriving at the house for a music lesson. After getting no reply, she knocked at the house of Mr Hughes, a neighbour of the Hinrichsons, and told him she thought something was wrong. Mr Hughes knocked several times, then looked through the parlour window. After seeing the same scenes of carnage that had sent the errand boy running for the police, Mr Hughes broke a window-pane and made a forced entry into the house. Within minutes, other people from the street were swarming into number 20, and when the policeman and the errand boy arrived at the scene, almost every inhabitant of Leveson Street was milling about near the house of horror.

Later that afternoon more policemen arrived to carry out a thorough search of the premises. The first body the police investigators encountered was that of Mrs Hinrichson. She was lying battered and stabbed in the hallway. In the parlour they found the maidservant, who was soaked in blood, having been battered about the head. She was barely alive. 5-year-old Henry, lying next to her, was not. Down in the cellar, the police discovered the small body of John. His throat had been cut from ear to ear. A bowl of bloodstained water was found in Wilson's room with a poker and tongs lying nearby, coated in blood. The motive for the killings had undoubtedly been robbery, as it was later established that a large sum of money belonging to the absent John Hinrichson had inexplicably gone missing.

Miss Parr was rushed to the Southern Hospital, where detectives waited for her to regain consciousness. She eventually came around, managed to recount what had taken place in the house that afternoon, then slipped into a coma.

For some unfathomable reason the killer went to Toxteth Park to wash his blood-spattered clothes in the park's figure-of-eight pit, in full view of a number of witnesses. From the park he made his way to a shop in London Road where he sold a gold watch. With the money from the sale he bought himself a pair of trousers from a clothes dealer in Great Homer Street, then went to his lodgings in Porter Street, where he asked his landlady for a clean shirt. The landlady gave Wilson one of her husband's shirts, and became suspicious when she saw that her lodger's discarded shirt was stained with blood.

At six that evening, Mr Wilson called at a barber's shop around the corner in Great Howard Street for a shave. While the barber was lathering his face, Wilson asked him if he had a wig to sell. The barber said he did not, but he knew of a shop in nearby Oil Street which supplied men's wigs, and he told Wilson that he would take him there if he wished. On the way to the shop, which was only three streets away, Wilson said to the barber, 'Have you heard about the murder?'

'No. What murder?' replied the barber.

'A terrible affair,' said Wilson. 'Two women and two children had their heads bashed in.'

'How awful!' said the barber, disgusted. 'Did they get him?'

'No, not yet,' replied Wilson.

After purchasing a wig, Wilson took a ferry ride across the Mersey and went to Tranmere to spend the night with his estranged wife. The following morning, however, despite knowing that a police dragnet had been thrown over the city to snare the country's most-wanted man, he again boarded a ferry and returned to Liverpool. Once across he visited the shop of Israel Samuel, a Great Howard Street watch dealer. Mr Samuel was an intuitive man, and he felt uneasy about Mr Wilson, who wanted £6 for a gold watch. Mr Samuel called for a policeman and asked him to examine the watch. The policeman said the watch did not resemble any that had been reported stolen, but still Mr Samuel felt there was something about Mr Wilson that he couldn't put his finger on. Mr Samuel told Wilson that he had insufficient cash on the premises to pay for the watch. But before Wilson left, the watch dealer told him that if he went with his son to his other shop in Dale Street, he would be given the money there. Wilson nodded, and Mr Samuel took his son to one side and in Hebrew said, 'When you are passing the police station, collar this fellow and give him in charge.'

And so, as Mr Samuel's son walked past the bridewell in Dale Street, he grabbed Wilson and took him in. Wilson was totally taken by surprise.

Around this time, Miss Mary Parr, the Hinrichsons' maidservant died without regaining consciousness.

After a lengthy interrogation, Wilson was thrown in a cell. In the days leading up to his trial, he often flew into fits of rage and screamed he was innocent.

He was tried at Liverpool Assizes on 23 August 1849, before Mr Justice Patterson, and without leaving their box, the jury found him guilty of the four murders. John Wilson, whose real name turned out to be Maurice Gleeson Wilson, was sentenced to death. On the Saturday morning of 15 September 1849 a crowd of 50,000 people from all over the region gathered to see the execution of Wilson at Kirkdale Gaol. At around 11.30 a.m. the crowd became quiet as a white dove suddenly descended from the blue skies and landed on the crossbeam of the scaffold. The bird stayed there eyeing the mob for a while until it was startled by the approach of two men: the prison governor and a priest.

The governor had come into the prison yard to explain the working of the scaffold to the priest, who wanted to be assured that the condemned man would have a swift, humane death.

Shortly before noon, Wilson was escorted by the under-sheriff from the condemned cell to the press room to meet the public executioner, a seventy-year-old hangman from York by the name of George Howard. Howard was very incompetent, and seemed more nervous than Wilson. He fumbled with the straps as he bound Wilson.

The condemned convict was escorted to the scaffold outside by two priests, who recited the litany for the dying. Wilson's face was suddenly white as a sheet and he began to pray. The executioner followed closely behind, occasionally displaying a prominent nervous twitch in his face.

Wilson was positioned on the drop. Howard slipped the noose over his head wrongly, and had to adjust it so the knot was on the right side of Wilson's neck. Howard then pulled the white cap over Wilson's head, but it was too small, and only managed to cover the top of his head, just to his eyebrows. Howard then retreated to the release lever, trembling. The clergymen, who had been standing on each side of Wilson, began to recite their prayers in raised voices, and moved back, away from the condemned man.

Howard triggered the mechanism that drew the bolt back, and the Leveson Street murderer fell two feet. A tremendous cheer went up from the crowd that faded as the spectators near to the execution witnessed Wilson's terrible death. Howard should have made the drop much longer than twenty-four inches. Wilson's death was slow and agonizing because of the old executioner's incompetence. He drew up his legs spasmodically, and because the white cap was not pulled over his face, some squeamish onlookers screamed and a few of them fainted as they saw Wilson's countenance become gruesomely distorted. His eyes bulged out of their sockets, and veins like purple knotted cords sprang up from his crimson cheeks. His elongated tongue hung out of his foaming mouth, and he made an awful choking sound. Howard suddenly reappeared and started pulling the white cap further down over the dying man's face, and Wilson's bulging eyes glanced sideways at the executioner in sheer horror, until they were finally covered. About fifteen minutes later, the hanged man stopped moving.

Ann Hinrichson, her unborn child and her two sons were buried along with Mary Parr in the same grave in nearby St. James's Cemetery.

Because of the notorious massacre associated with Leveson Street, crowds of morbid individuals made regular pilgrimages to see the house of blood at number 20. To dissuade the ghoulish sightseers from visiting the infamous street, the council later renamed the thoroughfare Grenville Street. Today Grenville Street South is the only vestige of a street that was once synonymous with murder.

6   Two Visions of Death

Most people find the idea of assassination vile, and in Britain there is, fortunately, a remarkable shortage of Lee Harvey Oswalds, although on several occasions in the nation's history, prominent individuals have been disposed of for religious and political reasons. In December 1710 Thomas à Becket, the Archbishop of Canterbury, was assassinated by Hugh de Merville, William de Tracy, Reginal Fitzurse and Richard le Breton, four of Henry II's knights. Becket was callously slayed because of his opposition to Henry's attempts to control the clergy.

Assassinations of British prime ministers have been exceptionally scarce since the days of Walpole, and in almost three centuries of British politics, only one chief minister of government has been killed by an assassin. His name was Spencer Perceval, and the man who took his life was a Liverpudlian named John Bellingham.

Spencer Perceval was born in 1762, the second son of the second Earl of Egmont. He was educated at Harrow and Trinity College, Cambridge, where he graduated with a Master of Arts in 1781. In 1783 Perceval's mother, the Baroness Arden died and left her fortune to her eldest son. Young Perceval struggled on, and studied hard to learn law at Lincoln's Inn. In 1786 he was called to the Bar, and soon obtained a reputation as a diligent and brief-hungry barrister. He also displayed a talent for voicing his strong political views, and in 1796 he entered Parliament as the Member for Northampton and became an ardent supporter of the Tory prime minister William Pitt. When Henry Addington succeeded Pitt as premier in 1801, he persuaded Perceval to join the new government as attorney general. Perceval worked hard at his new job, and when Pitt formed his second administration in 1804, Perceval kept his job. In 1807 the Duke of Portland became prime minister in the House of Lords, and Spencer Perceval was made chancellor of the exchequer, and in those days that meant he was also the leader of the House of Commons. In 1809 King George III, who thought highly of the new leader of the Commons and once called him 'the most straightforward man I have ever known' asked him to become prime minister, and Perceval accepted.

In the spring of 1812, a 42-year-old bankrupt Liverpool insurance broker named John Bellingham entered a gunsmith's shop in the Strand, London, and bought two pistols and ammunition for four guineas. Bellingham left the shop and headed for the wide-open spaces of Primrose Hill for a bit of shooting practice, before returning to his lodgings in New Millman Street.

Bellingham was a bitter and disillusioned man. He had once been involved in the lucrative business of exporting timber to Russia, but lost everything when a business contact went bankrupt. Unable to pay the resulting mammoth debts, Bellingham was thrown in prison. Upon his release, he visited Russia and complained to the authorities with such vigour that they imprisoned him too. Bellingham repeatedly wrote to the British ambassador to intervene on his behalf and secure his release, but the ensuing tangle of British and Soviet red tape achieved nothing, and Bellingham remained in a cold Russian prison cell for months.

When he was finally released, Bellingham returned to England and began a feverish campaign to get his case reviewed; he also demanded compensation. He wrote countless indignant letters to his MP and even informed the Prince Regent of his unjust incarceration. But all the protests came to nothing, and no redress was made. Once, Bellingham stormed into Whitehall and demanded action, but he met a wall of unsympathetic officialdom. At the top of his voice he told one Whitehall official that he was going to take legal action against the government as a result of its wanton neglect; the official roared back, 'Go to the Devil!'

So John Bellingham decided to vent his anger at British bureaucracy by shooting the prime minister, preferably in the House of Commons and in the presence of all its members. But first he would have to do a bit of reconnoitring at the scene of the intended crime. Thereafter he made it his daily habit to visit the Commons, where he lurked about the central lobby, observing the route the prime minister took when entering the Chamber. He also became a frequent visitor to the Commons coffee room.

And now for a strange supernatural twist to this tale ...

On the night of 3 May a Mr John Williams, who was a banker of Redruth, Cornwall, had a vivid dream in which he found himself standing in the lobby of the House of Commons. In this dream he saw a small man dressed in a blue coat and white waistcoat enter the lobby. Moments later, another man in a snuff-coloured coat with yellow metal buttons suddenly drew a small pistol and fired it at the man in blue. The dream was so realistic that the sleeping Mr Williams could actually discern the ball from the pistol striking the left side of the victim's chest, where it left a neat little spot. Shocked by the incident, the dreamer turned to a group of other people in the lobby and asked them who had been shot; someone replied that it was the prime minister, Spencer Perceval. The bystanders then charged at the murderer to apprehend him.

At this point in the dream, Mr Williams awoke and gave an account of the strange dream to his wife. She assured him that it was only a nightmare and Mr Williams went back to sleep but the same disturbing dream replayed in his mind two more times that night.

The following morning Mr Williams began to think about the significance of the recurring dream, and wondered if he ought to travel to London to warn Mr Perceval. Later at work he related the previous night's events to several business acquaintances and asked them for advice. His friends told him that he would be ridiculed as a madman if he were to go to London on the strength of a mere dream, so Mr Williams decided not to make the trip. All the same, he scanned *The Times* each day to see if there had been any shooting incidents at Westminster.

On the afternoon of Monday 11 May Spencer Perceval left 10 Downing Street and, seeing it was a nice sunny day, he dismissed his carriage and set off to the House on foot. At around 5.15 p.m. Perceval entered the lobby of the House, and a few seconds later Bellingham drew his pistol from his right-hand breeches pocket. He stepped out from behind a pillar, raised his pistol, aimed it at Perceval, and in full view of all the constituents, he fired. The ball blasted a small neat hole in the left side of the prime minister's chest. Perceval cried, 'Murder!' and staggered three paces; then he fell on his side and rolled face down on to the floor. Mr Goodiff, an officer of the house attacked the assassin, grabbed his arm and restrained him. He asked Bellingham if he had shot the prime minister, and Bellingham replied, 'I am the unhappy man who has shot Mr Perceval. My name is John Bellingham. I know what I have done. It was a private injury, a denial of justice on the part of the government.'

Bellingham was instantly recognized by Sir Banastre Tarleton and Mr Gascoyne, two Liverpool MPs who were in the Lobby at the time. Gascoyne also sprung upon Bellingham and twisted his arm while someone removed the smoking pistol from his hand. The assassin was then body-searched, and the second pistol was found on him.

Meanwhile Perceval was carried into the nearby office of the Speaker's secretary and laid on a sofa. When Doctor Lynn of Great Smith Street arrived ten minutes later, he found he could do nothing. Perceval was dead.

All the doors of the House were locked and Bellingham was taken along several private passages to the prison rooms in the upper storey of the Commons, where he was interrogated by the Cabinet council for over seven hours.

Perceval's body was taken to his wife and five children, who were devastated by the killing.

News of the murder travelled quickly across the nation, and there were many in the upper echelons of British society who believed that the assassination was but the starting shot of the long-awaited British Revolution. Paranoid aristocrats shuddered, remembering the Revolution across the channel in France that had occurred a mere two decades earlier. The social unrest among the poverty-stricken lower classes, fuelled by introduction of machines into the workplace, seemed ready to explode any day, and the riotous activities of the Luddites were becoming increasingly organized. To make matters worse, the country's economy was at an all-time low because of the cost of the Napoleonic Wars. But one individual who learned of the assassination was more dumbfounded than shocked. He was Mr Williams of Cornwall, the man who had foreseen the shooting in a recurring dream. He immediately travelled to London, and purchased a tinted etching of the prime minister's murder, and was astounded to see that every detail of the drawing was identical to the details he had witnessed in his dream – from the colours of the coats to the exact position of the gunshot wound in the victim's chest.

Following his interrogation in the House, Bellingham was taken under a strong guard of Dragoons to a waiting hackney coach in the Lower Palace Yard outside. By this time the crowds had swelled, and when they saw the tall gaunt figure of Bellingham, they shouted 'Burdett for ever!'

The mob was referring to Sir Francis Burdett, a popular politician of the time who had been imprisoned for advocating freedom of speech, Catholic emancipation, and other liberal measures. As Bellingham entered the coach, several of the more daring members of the crowd attempted to give him a chance of escape by trying to open the opposite door of the carriage, but a party of Life Guards suddenly arrived and formed a semicircle around the coach. Moments later, the coach trundled across the yard and made its way to Newgate Prison.

Bellingham was tried on 15 May and it took the jury only fifteen minutes to return a verdict of guilty. He was sentenced to death by hanging, and while he waited for the 18th, his execution date, the condemned prisoner sat in his cell writing letters to his wife in Duke Street, Liverpool, assuring her that he would be coming home in a day or two.

On the Monday morning of 18 May at twenty minutes past seven, the lord mayor, sheriffs and a twenty-strong crowd of other notables arrived at Newgate to see the sentence of law executed. The usual throng of necrophiles and various sensation-seekers looked on from window seats and rooftops overlooking the gallows – indeed any vantage point that afforded a decent view of the execution scene. At 7.30 a.m. Bellingham came down from his cell with the Reverend Doctor Ford to have his irons knocked off. The two men were then joined by the major and sheriffs, and they all walked into the press yard where the condemned had to wait in the rain until he was instructed to approach the scaffold. Shortly after Bellingham's wrists were tied together, and a rope was tied around both arms at waist level. At this point a tear trickled down John Bellingham's face, and he told the executioner to make the noose tight to ensure 'no inconvenience'. He ascended the steps of the scaffold with the reverend, and some members of the crowd started shouting 'Hurrah!' But a far greater number retorted by shouting 'Silence!'

The rope was fastened around Bellingham's neck and the white cap was placed on his head. At this point the reverend started to pray with Bellingham for a while, then asked him how he felt. Calmly and rationally Bellingham said he thanked God for having enabled him to meet his fate with so much fortitude and resignation.

The executioner put the white linen hood over the condemned man's head, and Bellingham objected. But Reverend Ford told the condemned man he would have to wear it. The hood was tied around the lower part of Bellingham's face with a white handkerchief. The crowd started to chant 'God bless you' over and over, then a terrible silence descended on the scene. The executioner went below the scaffold and got ready to strike away the supports of the trapdoor that Bellingham was standing on. The clock struck 8 a.m., and on the seventh chime, the executioner removed the supports with one skilful blow, and John Bellingham dropped. His death was swift, because the executioner had decided to pull the hanged man's legs to speed the process of neck-breaking strangulation.

The body was left to hang until 9 a.m., when it was cut down and put on a cart and covered with a sack. The executioner's assistant and a boy took the cart to St

Bartholomew's Hospital, where it was dissected before a ghoulish gaggle of public spectators.

One hundred and sixty-eight years later another assassination took place, but this time a Liverpool man was not the assassin, but the victim, and this killing was also said to have been foreseen.

On 8 September 1980, and American psychic named Alex Tanous was being interviewed by Lee Spiegel for NBC radio's *Unexplained Phenomena* show. The interview was going out live and was being held in the office of the American Society for Psychical Research, which is located on West 73rd Street in New York City.

Spiegel asked Tanous to prove his alleged powers of second sight by making a prediction, preferably one that would be of particular interest to the radio station's audience, who belonged to the eighteen to thirty-five age group. Tanous paused for a moment, as if concentrating, then said, 'A very famous rock star will have an untimely death, and this can happen from this moment on. I say "untimely" because there is something strange about this death, but it will affect the consciousness of many people because of his fame. The star will be foreign-born but living in the United States.'

After giving his prediction, Tanous glanced through the windows of his office at the building opposite, a superior high-rise known as the Dakota Apartments.

Three months later, on the night of 8 December, a limousine pulled up outside the Dakota Apartments building at 10.50 p.m., and Yoko Ono left the vehicle. Her husband John Lennon followed her a few moments later, clutching several reels of tape from a recording session on which he'd been working. As John walked under the archway leading to the Dakota building, he heard a voice behind him call out, 'Mr Lennon.'

John turned to see tubby 25-year-old Mark Chapman a

mere twenty feet away, crouched in a combat stance and pointing a .38 Undercover Special handgun. A heartbeat later Chapman pumped four hollow-point bullets into one of Liverpool's most famous and adored sons. The songwriter who urged the world's leaders to 'give peace a chance' staggered up the steps of the building's entrance and fell flat on his face. Minutes later John was placed on the back seat of a police car which rushed him to the nearest hospital with its roof-lights flashing and its siren screaming. As the police car jumped the traffic lights on Broadway, police officer James Moran, who had been a Beatles fan in his youth, leaned back and talked to John Lennon in a vain attempt to keep him conscious. Moran was deeply shocked at the shooting, but to his dying idol he managed to say, 'Are you John Lennon?'

With his life rapidly ebbing away, John faintly replied, 'Yes.'

And that was the last word John Lennon uttered. He was the 701st person to be gunned down in New York City that year.

Chapman is currently serving a 'twenty years to life' sentence at Attica State Prison in northern New York State. He is kept in solitary confinement to prevent any of the prison's other 2,000 inmates from attacking him. He may be eligible for parole around the year 2001.

Chapman's motive for killing the ex-Beatle is still unclear. The official theory was that Chapman was simply a psychotic Lennon fanatic trying to make a name for himself, but there is something more sinister about the killing. Chapman was dismissed as a 'lone nut' – the same expression that was used to describe Lee Harvey Oswald seventeen years earlier in Dallas, Texas. In fact the murder of John Lennon has several striking parallels with that of John F. Kennedy. When Lennon's body was taken to the morgue, the gunshot wounds in the cadaver were so close together that one pathologist remarked,

'Good shot group' – which is a firing-range term used by the police and the military to describe skilled marksmanship. Yet Chapman was said to be a novice with firearms. But the grouping of the gunshot wounds in Lennon's body was so tight that pathologists at the morgue got mixed up trying to count them as they conducted their post-mortem.

The assassin's choice of weapon, the Undercover Special, known on the street as a 'Saturday night special', is an extremely reliable gun. It is deadly accurate and never jams or misfires, yet is small and sleek enough to fit into the back pocket of your jeans. In May 1972 would-be assassin Arthur Bremner used one to blast Alabama Governor George C. Wallace: the bullet that impacted into the politician's spine left him wheelchair-bound for life.

Besides the mystery of Chapman's expert choice of weapon and his inexplicable marksmanship, there is the fuzzy account of the killer's journey from his home in Honolulu to New York that just doesn't stand up to the most cursory examination. According to the official version of events, Mark Chapman persuaded his wife to take out a loan of $2,500 from her employer's credit union, and without her knowledge he used this sum to finance the assassination. He bought his well-chosen gun and dum-dum bullets, and flew overnight from Honolulu to New York on a United Airlines plane. But the distinguished British barrister Fenton Bresler, who researched the Lennon murder for eight years, unearthed a plethora of sinister missing links. Firstly, he discovered that United Airlines had no direct flights from Honolulu to New York. One actually has to fly by way of Chicago. Chapman did not mention this. Further investigations made by Bresler convinced the barrister that the killer spent three unaccounted-for days in Chicago. Bresler got in touch with the New York County district attorney's office and told them about the three 'missing' days, but they denied that the facts had any substance. Bresler believes that the days in question – from 2 to 5 December – were covered up by the authorities. During that period, he claims, Chapman was probably being 'programmed' to kill by the CIA with brainwashing drugs and repeated hypnotic suggestion. Is Bresler right? Was there a top-level conspiracy to assassinate John Lennon? Let us examine some less-publicized facts about one of Liverpool's most famous sons.

The FBI and the CIA had files on Lennon dating back to the 1960s that detail the star's participation in anti-war demos. There are two reports in one dossier on Lennon for May 1972 with the heading 'Revolutionary Activities'. The FBI and CIA apparently saw Lennon as a cult-like leader who had the latent ability to overthrow the established government of the United States; a political subversive who could easily produce a song along the lines of 'Power to the People' to incite millions of Americans to demonstrate against the reactionary policies of the newly elected president Ronald Reagan. As early as 1972 Lennon knew he was under constant surveillance. He said at the time to reporters, 'I'd open the door. There'd be guys on the other side of the street. I'd get into my car, and they'd be following me in a car. Not hiding. They wanted me to see that I was being followed.'

By September 1973 Lennon's telephone was bugged, a fact to which even the Justice Department later admitted. In December 1975 Lennon said, 'We knew we were being wire-tapped. There was a helluva lot of guys coming in to fix the phones.'

In the light of these cloak-and-dagger details, Bresler's conspiracy theory seems less outlandish. Furthermore the week John Lennon was shot he was due to fly to San

Francisco to participate in a rally for Japanese–
American workers on strike. He was so enthusiastic to
get to the demonstration, he had already bought the
airline tickets.

In November 1992 Mark Chapman broke his silence
over the Lennon murder when he agreed to be
interviewed by American television reporter Barbara
Walters in Attica State prison. Chapman dismissed the
commonly held belief that he had killed John Lennon to
become famous. He also told Walters that he was
horrified by the amount of fan-mail he regularly received
from people wanting his autograph.

'That tells you something is truly sick in our society,'
Chapman told Walters in a broken voice.

7 The Way to a Man's Heart

She was a pretty young auburn-haired woman from Mobile, Alabama, and he was a wealthy middle-aged businessman from the respectable Liverpool suburb of Aigburth. She was 18-year-old Florence Chandler, and he was 42-year-old James Maybrick, and it was upon the luxurious White Star liner *Britannic* in the year 1881 that their paths through life met.

The Liverpool-bound liner was moving across the icy expanses of the mid Atlantic when James Maybrick first set eyes upon Miss Chandler, who was travelling alone. He approached her and introduced himself, and when she spoke, Mr Maybrick found her accent quaintly indeterminable. It seemed to contain elements of upper-class English and a hint of the Continental with an intonation redolent of the American South. Miss Chandler explained that her hybrid accent was the result of a cosmopolitan upbringing. During her formative years she had lived with various relatives in London, Paris and the other major European cities, as well as New York, where she had just been to see her grandmother. The faint Southern drawl was the legacy of a childhood spent in the sunny cotton fields of Alabama.

When Maybrick mentioned he was from Liverpool, Miss Chandler said she had been to the city to see the world-famous Grand National at Aintree, and she began to talk of horsemanship, which by coincidence was one of Mr Maybrick's main interests.

Seven days later James Maybrick announced his engagement to Miss Chandler to the rest of the liner's passengers, and when the captain of the *Britannic* learned of the betrothal, he rang the ship's bell and proposed a toast to the couple's future.

Later that year, in July, the couple were married in London at St James's Church, Piccadilly, and they enjoyed a honeymoon in Brazil.

For several years the couple lived at Norfolk, Virginia, where Mr Maybrick conducted his business as a cotton-broker. Every morning he would leave Florence, who by now had a baby boy to look after, and head for his office at the Norfolk Cotton Exchange. But, unknown to his wife, James Maybrick did not always to directly to work. Most mornings he made little detours to various drug stores along Main Street to purchase arsenic, which he took regularly in small quantities, because he believed it fortified him.

On one occasion Maybrick was preparing a meal for himself when a friend saw him adding a grey powder to the food. When his friend asked him what the powder was, Maybrick casually replied, 'It is arsenic. We all take some poison more or less. For instance I am now taking enough arsenic to kill you. I take this once in a while because I find it strengthens me.'

In 1884 the Maybricks returned to England and took up residence at Battlecrease House, in Aigburth's Riversdale road. James Maybrick continued to prosper in his business, and he and Florance moved upwards into the exclusive circles of Liverpool's high society. They attended countless soirées, dances, dinner parties, horse races and numerous public events held at St George's Hall.

In 1886 Florence gave birth to a second child, a daughter named Gladys Evelyn, But the joy the new child brought was cut short when an epidemic of scarlatina hit Liverpool. Five-year-old James Maybrick, the elder child, was stricken with the fever. Because his father feared that his baby daughter would also contract the fever, he and a nursemaid took her to Wales, leaving Florence to tend little James. For six weeks Florence cared for her son and, in the end, thanks to her dedication, he pulled through.

But around this time, Florence was devastated to learn from one of the staff at Battlecrease House that her husband had a mistress somewhere in Liverpool and that, long before his marriage, this woman had given birth to two of his children. And since their marriage, the woman had borne him a third child, Florence was told.

When James Maybrick returned to Battlecrease House, Florence did not confront him, but acted as if everything were normal. Not that her husband would have noticed anyway. He began to stay out late, and often told Florence he would be going to London on business, but she found she could no longer trust him. She spent many interminable and lonely nights sitting in the drawing room, wondering where her husband really was. He had become a stranger to her. Then one night when he returned home late, she told him she could no longer sleep in the same bed as him.

In December 1888 the Maybricks were entertaining a number of guests at their home, one of whom in particular viewed Florence with an amorous eye. He was a tall handsome thirty-eight-year-old bachelor named Alfred Brierley, a wealthy cotton broker who had offices in New Orleans and Liverpool, and who came from a prominent Lancashire family. Standing head and shoulders above the other guests, Brierley quickly caught the attention of Florence, who found him very charming.

Brierley was invited back many times and became a frequent dinner guest at the house of the Maybricks. During the following March Brierley often accompanied James and Florence Maybrick to the early spring horse races. As the weeks went by it was clear that Florence was becoming increasingly fond of Brierley, and vice versa. While James Maybrick was in London on business, Alfred Brierley visited Florence and declared his love for her. He asked her to go away with him. Florence tried to hold back her feelings for a while, then relented. She later spent three days with Brierley at Flatman's Hotel in London's Cavendish Square, posing as his wife.

Florence returned from her little sojourn on 28 March, and on the following day she accompanied her husband to Aintree for the Grand National. Among the crowd of racegoers was Alfred Brierley. Florence blushed and gave a tell-tale smile, which drove her husband wild with jealousy. To make matters worse, Brierley approached the Maybricks and asked Florence if she would like to see the Prince of Wales. Florence nodded and took his arm. The two smiled at each other under Florence's parasol and walked towards the grandstand.

Later that day at Battlecrease House, James Maybrick gave his wife a black eye during a fierce altercation over the Brierley incident, and Florence said enough was enough. She said she was leaving immediately. But James warned that if she did leave him, he would never allow her to see the children again. Florence walked to the hall, confused by her divided loyalties, and Maybrick roared, 'By heavens, Florie, if you cross this doorstep you shall never enter this house again!'

Reluctantly Mrs Maybrick turned on her heel and in tears was led by the children's nanny to the nursery where the baby was crying.

The following morning she sought the advice of the

family physician, Dr Arthur Hopper. She told him of her husband's brutal attack on her, and, as Dr Hopper examined her black eye, she said she intended to see if a separation could be arranged. But the doctor tried to dissuade her, promising that he would drop in at Battlecrease House to see Mr Maybrick about his deplorable behaviour.

About a week afterwards Alfred Brierley received a letter from Florence, uring him to visit her without delay. When Brierley arrived he was shocked to see that Florence had a black eye, and she told him about the beating she had received after returning home from the Grand National. Although visibly upset by the barbaric treatment Florence had received from her husband, he offered no remedy and no support whatsoever. This was another bitter blow to Florence.

On 13 April James Maybrick boarded a train for London, where he intended to spend the weekend with his brother, Michael, before consulting Dr Charles Fuller about the state of his health. Maybrick was something of a hypochondriac, and was continually preoccupied with the fear that every ache and pain heralded the onset of creeping paralysis. Ironically his few genuine health problems were caused by the arsenical medications he was forever taking for this imaginary disease.

Dr Fuller examined Maybrick and informed him that the symptoms he described indicated nothing more serious than dyspepsia, a mere stomach upset. Maybrick was very relieved to hear this, and returned to Liverpool in an optimistic mood on 22 April.

A couple of days after his return Florence Maybrick went to the local chemist shop of Thomas Wokes and bought a dozen fly-papers. She told the proprietor that the flies in her kitchen were getting out of hand. Mr Wokes smiled, rolled up the fly-papers and handed them to the delivery boy. Mrs Maybrick paid him sixpence, then returned home, ahead of the delivery boy.

Several days later two servants were curious to see a towel covering something in Mrs Maybrick's room. One of them lifted the towel and saw a basin. In the basin was a small bowl also covered by a towel. This towel was lifted to reveal several fly-papers soaking in a bowl of water. In those days fly-papers contained significant amounts of arsenic; knowing this, the curious servants became quite suspicious. Two days later James Maybrick was coming downstairs when he experience a distressing spell of dizziness. After the spell lifted, Maybrick proceeded to his office in the city. He arrived at the Knowsley Buildings shortly after 10.30 a.m., and to his colleagues he complained of stiffness in his legs. That afternoon Maybrick tried to shake off his symptoms. He went across the Mersey to see the horse races on the Wirral. When he arrived his face was a sickly white, and several racetrack friends told him that he looked quite unwell.

When Maybrick got home to Battlecrease House, he was sweating profusely. He went to bed, and when he awoke the next morning, he found his condition was the same, so Doctor Humphreys, who was the children's doctor and the physician who lived nearest to the house, was summoned.

When the doctor arrived, Mrs Maybrick told him about the white powder her husband had a habit of taking, and the doctor quizzed Maybrick about his arsenic addiction.

Later that day Mr Maybrick's health improved slightly, and he enjoyed a bowl of oxtail soup. Maybrick's health was now on the mend, and on 30 April he no longer needed his wife to nurse him, so she took a break from her duties and attended a ball in Wavertree.

On Mayday James Maybrick was back to his usual self and seemed to have made a complete recovery. Until he tried to eat. For the more he took food, the more nauseous he felt. Suddenly, on 3 May, Maybrick suffered a relapse, and his condition started to worsen to such an alarming extent, that Florence called for Dr William Carter, a prominent Rodney Street practitioner. When Dr Carter arrived, he was escorted to Mr Maybrick's bedroom and found his patient in a sorry state. Maybrick was writhing from stomach pains, and had been vomiting. Dr Carter examined him and concluded that he was suffering from acute dyspepsia, and he assured Florence that her husband would be right as rain in a few days.

That same afternoon Alice Yapp, the children's nanny, spotted Florence pouring medicine from one bottle into another in a rather furtive manner. The nurse found this very suspicious, and on the following day, she decided to root through Mrs Maybrick's things. In a trunk belonging to her mistress, the nanny discovered a packet labelled 'arsenic'. This was the proof Nurse Yapp needed to confirm her suspicion. She immediately told Mrs Matilda Briggs, an old friend of Mr Maybrick, about the find. Then the motive behind the misdeed was discovered on the afternoon of 8 May, when Mrs Maybrick gave Nurse Yapp a letter to post. This letter was addressed to A. Brierley, Esq, 60 Huskisson Street, Liverpool. According to Nurse Yapp, on the way to the post office, she gave the letter to Mrs Maybrick's baby daughter, Gladys, and Gladys dropped the letter in some mud. As a result the nurse said she transferred the letter from the sullied envelope to a new clean one that she had bought from the post office earlier. In the process Nurse Yapp said she couldn't help noticing that Mrs Maybrick had described her husband's condition in the letter as 'sick unto death'. Considering the fact that Mr Maybrick was only supposed to be suffering from dyspepsia, the phrase struck her as odd, to say the least. Nurse Yapp also noticed that Mrs Maybrick addressed Alfred Brierley as 'my own darling' in the letter.

Mrs Briggs told Mr Maybrick's brothers Edwin and Michael what she suspected, and the two men set off for Battlecrease House to investigate. When they arrived, Edwin showed his brother the letter that Nurse Yapp had opened. After a quick scan, Michael said, 'The woman is an adulteress.'

When they went upstairs, they were shocked at the poor state of their brother. Michael visited Dr Humphreys' house that night and told him about the fly-papers in the bowl and how Nurse Yapp suspected Mrs Maybrick of poisoning her husband. But Dr Humphreys refused to take the allegation seriously.

At 8.30 p.m. on 11 May James Maybrick died, surrounded by his family and friends. But Florence was not there. Earlier that day around 11 a.m. she had fainted from the exhaustion brought on by the long hours spent at her sick husband's bedside and was lying in a semi-conscious state on the bed in the dressing room when Mr Maybrick expired.

Later that night Nurse Yapp discovered a brown paper parcel and a chocolate box. In the box were two bottles labelled 'arsenic', and the words, 'poison for cats' had been written on the label in red ink by someone. The brown paper parcel contained a yellowish powder. The brothers told a solicitor about the find, and he advised them to keep any evidence in a safe place, so they locked the chocolate box and the parcel in the wine cellar.

Garston police were later notified, and were told that the circumstances surrounding Mr Maybrick's death were suspicious. An Inspector Baxendale soon turned up and interviewed the Maybrick brothers, Mrs Briggs and all of the servants, before viewing Mr Maybrick's body. Baxendale heard of their suspicions regarding Florence, and the next day, Michael Maybrick took the package of arsenic found by Miss Yapp from the locked cellar and handed it over to the inspector. That same day

Superintendent Isaac Bryning instructed his men to take samples from the drains of Battlecrease House in case there were traces of arsenic lying in the sediments.

The revelations of the post-mortem that took place at five o'clock that afternoon strengthened the suspicions of the Maybrick brothers and Nurse Yapp. The lining of Maybrick's stomach was dappled with black patches, and the duodenum was scarlet with severe inflammation. Dr Alexander Barron, a professor of Pathology, and Dr Humphreys carried out the autopsy, and Dr Carter took notes throughout. Maybrick's stomach was removed and placed in a jar, which was sealed, then handed to Inspector Baxendale.

According to Dr Barron, Maybrick's death was due to acute inflammation of the stomach which in turn had been caused by an irritant poison.

On 14 May Florence Maybrick was arrested, taken to the local police station in Lark Lane, then escorted to Walton Jail. A female warder took Mrs Maybrick's valuables, then led her to a cell in the prison's hospital.

The trial opened at St George's Hall on 31 July and lasted for seven days. The servants of Battlecrease House gave their damning evidence, as did Michael Maybrick and the various chemists who innocently supplied Florence with her deadly doses of arsenic. And all this evidence was crowned by a Dr Stevenson, the Home Office expert on toxins, who stated categorically that Mr Maybrick had died of arsenic poisoning. And so on the final day of the trial at 3.56 p.m., the clerk of arraigns looked at the sombre jury and asked, 'Have you agreed upon a verdict, gentlemen?'

The foreman of the jury, a Mr Wainwright, replied, 'We have.'

'And do you find the prisoner guilty of the murder of James Maybrick or not guilty?'

'Guilty,' said Mr Wainwright, and a wave of sighs rose from the gallery.

Florence trembled slightly, and buried her face in her hands.

The clerk of arraigns said, 'Florence Elizabeth Maybrick, you have been found guilty of wilful murder. Have you anything to say why the court should not pronounce sentence upon you?'

Florence rose from her seat in the dock and held the rail to steady herself. She bowed to his lordship, then replied, 'My lord, everything has been against me. Although evidence has been given as to a great many circumstances in connection with Mr Brierley, much has been withheld which might have influenced the jury had it been told. I am not guilty of this crime.'

Moments later the judge donned the black silk cap and read the death sentence. The sound of sobs and sniffles from several women echoed through the court. Florence sat in the dock crying like a child.

When news of the verdict reached the huge crowd assembled outside St George's Hall, their hisses could be heard along the length of Lime Street. Later, when several servants who had given evidence emerged from St George's Hall, a rabble-rouser in the waiting throng mistakenly identified one of them as Nurse Yapp, and the crowd became agitated to such an extent that seventy policeman were summoned. As the servants were herded into a cab, the mob bombarded them with profanities. Later, when the judge that sentenced Mrs Maybrick left St George's Hall under a heavy police guard, the same wild crowd jeered him and attacked the carriage into which he was rather keenly climbing. When the carriage finally managed to escape from the thronged courtyard, a chant of 'Shame! Shame!' started.

About an hour later the crowd had still not disbanded, and mounted police had to be brought in to prepare the exit route for the prison van that was to take Florence Maybrick to the gallows of Walton Jail. Florence was taken to the van, and as soon as the vehicle started to move through the courtyard, a tremendous cheer swelled up, and did not fade until the van was lost to the sight of the crowd.

At Walton Florence was put in the condemned cell. The day of her execution was to be Monday 26 August. Long before the dreaded date Florence heard the terrifying sounds of sawing and hammering that signified the erection of the gallows.

But beyond the prison walls, an astounding turn of events was taking shape. A majority of the people in Britain and abroad thought that the Maybrick verdict was grossly unjust, and the home secretary was inundated with countless petittions for a reprieve. (The idea of a woman being hanged enraged many people in Victorian times.) But time was starting to run out.

Four days before the execution date, Florence was walking in Walton's prison yard when Mr Anderson, the governor of the jail, called her name as he approached.

He said, 'Maybrick, no commutation of sentence has come down today, and I consider it is my duty to tell you to prepare for death.'

Florence replied, 'Thank you, governor. My conscience is clear. God's will be done.'

That night Florence Maybrick said her prayers and went to bed. At 1.30 a.m. she woke to the cacophony of wheels trundling over the courtyard outside. It was the cab of the Queen's messenger, who had come from London with good news. Moments later a key rattled in the lock of her cell door, and Florence sat up in bed, waiting anxiously. The prison governor entered with the chaplain and a warder. Florence listened in dreamy disbelief as the governor excitedly told her that she had been reprieved.

Florence's sentence was commuted to life imprisonment, and she spent fifteen years as prisoner P29 in the jails of Aylesbury and Woking, and did not enjoy freedom until July 1904. After her release Florence travelled to Rouen to be reunited with her mother, the Baroness von Roques. Towards the end of August that year Florence decided to return to the United States. Months after her emotional homecoming she wrote a book of her experience in prison entitled, *My Fifteen Lost Years*.

Florence later dropped her famous (some would say infamous) surname and replaced it with her maiden name, Chandler. Thereafer she shunned all publicity, becoming something of an eccentric recluse. She moved to Florida, then to Illinois, before finally spending her last days in an anonymous little shack among the woodlands of Connecticut.

In 1927 she made a final visit to Liverpool to attend the Grand National. On 24 October 1941 Florence was found dead in her little cabin. She was eighty-one years old.

8 Jack the Ripper's
Liverpool Connection

Five times he struck, then disappeared off the face of the earth, leaving nothing but a legendary nickname and a mystery over which generations of professional and amateur criminologists would argue forever after. I am of course referring to the anonymous Victorian serial killer, nicknamed Jack the Ripper, also known as the Whitechapel Murderer and the East End Terror.

Jack killed five prostitutes in and around the Whitechapel district of London over a period of four months in 1888. After the murders came to an abrupt halt in November 1888, the police were embarrassed by their failure to capture Jack. Meawhile the British public were beginning to regard the enigmatic Jack as a sort of folklore hero who had managed to escape the establishment's retribution; a sneering rogue who had cunningly flouted the repressed conventions of Victorian society in a shocking and brutal way. As soon as Jack reached this kind of elevated status, he became the subject of intense study and 'Rippermania' hit the nation. Stories regarding the murderer's identity began to circulate. The names of prominent persons, including a royal surgeon, famous sportsmen and even members of the clergy, were whispered in the quest for a prime suspect. Countless landlords and landladies in the East End were certain that one of their lodgers had been the Whitechapel Murderer, and just as many policemen could recall how they had chased the fleeting silhouette of Jack through the gaslit labyrinth of alleyways. Alas the murderer was always one step ahead.

But among all the tales of the Ripper, there are some stories that are apparently based on genuine facts. Over the years there have been many rumours alleging that the Ripper had connections with Liverpool. The origin of these rumours is probably the two letters that were sent from Merseyside to Scotland Yard at the height of the murder investigation by someone claiming to be Jack the Ripper. These letters were dismissed as the work of a crank by the police, but in the light of information that was not available to Scotland Yard at the time of the murders, many Ripperologists now think the letters were genuine. I will discuss this in greater detail later, but first here are the facts about the Whitechapel Murders.

At 3.40 a.m. on the dark autumnal morning of Friday 31 August 1888 a carter named Charles Cross of Bethnal Green was walking through Bucks Row (nowadays called Durward Street), Whitechapel, on his way to work, when he noticed what he thought was a bundle of tarpaulin that had fallen off a cart lying at the entrance of a stable yard. When he looked closer, Cross saw that the 'bundle' was in fact a woman lying on her back. Her skirts and petticoat had been pulled up above her waist, and from this Cross concluded that the woman had been raped. Another carter suddenly emerged out of the darkness. His name was Robert Paul, and when he saw Cross bending over the inert body, his gait slowed. Cross said to him, 'Come and look at this woman.'

Paul walked over to Cross, and when the latter suggested that they should lift the woman to her feet,

Paul shook his head and bent down to feel the woman's hands and face. They were stone cold.

'She's dead. We'd better get a policeman,' said Paul.

Before the carters left the deceased woman, Paul made her decent by rolling her skirt back down. The two men then rushed off in search for a police constable. On the corner of Hanbury Street, they found PC Mizen and informed him of their gruesome discovery. When the policeman reached the scene of the crime, he discovered that a colleague, PC Neil, was already there, sweeping the beam of his lamp over the woman's corpse. The light of his torch revealed that the dead woman's throat had been cut from ear to ear, and the blood from the wound had run into the gutter. A local doctor, Ralph Llewellyn, was instantly notified of the murder and arrived soon afterwards to examine the body by torchlight. The doctor officially pronounced life extinct, then ordered the removal of the body to the Whitechapel Mortuary. When the body was stripped naked in preparation for the post-mortem examination, it became sickenly evident that the woman had not only had her throat cut; her abdomen had also been savagely ripped open – to such an extent that her intestines were hanging out. There were also several stab wounds around the genitals and bruises on the right side of the jaw. Doctor Llewellyn expressed the opinion that the ripping of the woman's abdomen had killed her, and that the cutting of her throat had been carried out after her death. From the pattern of the jagged incisions that ran from the bottom of the woman's ribs to her lower abdomen, the doctor deduced that the murderer was left-handed, possessed a basic knowledge of human anatomy, and had probably used a long-bladed knife.

The victim of this hideous crime was later identified as Mary Ann Nichols, a 42-year-old poverty-stricken prostitute who lived in Whitechapel's run-down Thrawl

Street. Apart from the murderer, the last person to see Nichols alive was her friend, Ellen Holland, who had been a fellow lodger in the same doss-house. Holland said she had met Nichols, who was in a drunken state, at about 2.30 a.m. on the morning of the murder, and had tried to persuade her to return to their lodgings. But Nichols walked off into the darkness, looking for a client.

Eight days later, on Saturday 8 September, the Whitechapel Murderer (as he was now known) struck again. The second victim, 47-year-old Annie Chapman, was also a prostitute. Her body was discovered next to a fence in the backyard of a barber's shop at 29 Hanbury Street by John Davis, a market porter. Chapman had been completely disembowelled and her throat had been cut so savagely that the knife had passed right through her neck scarf, leaving the head almost severed from the body. Her small intestine had been positioned over her left shoulder, and at her feet the murderer had meticulously arranged the victim's rings and several coins in a neat line. The post-mortem revealed that Chapman's uterus was missing.

The murders generated a wave of terror that swept through London's East End. A rumour spread that the killer was a mad doctor who carried his knives in a little black bag, which incited gangs of vigilantes to hound scores of innocent doctors who made house-calls with such bags.

Then out of the blue, on 29 September, a letter arrived in London at the Central News Agency. Written in a mocking, taunting style, the letter began: 'Dear Boss, I keep hearing the police have caught me but they wont fix me just yet. I have laughed when they look so clever and talk about being on the right track.'

And the writer of the letter threatened: 'I am down on whores and I shant quit ripping them till I do get buckled.'

The disturbing epistle ended with the request: 'Keep this letter back till I do a bit more work, then give it out straight. My knife's nice and sharp and I want to get back to work right away if I get a chance. Good luck.'

The letter was signed: 'Yours truly, Jack the Ripper,' and a sardonic postscript beneath the infamous signature read: 'Don't mind me giving the trade name.'

The News Agency decided to withhold the letter as Jack had instructed, and waited in suspense for further developments. They didn't have to wait long. At one o'clock on the following morning Louis Diemschutz, a steward of the local Socialist Club, was leading his pony and cart into the backyard of the club where he worked in Berner Street, Whitechapel, when suddenly the animal stopped, evidently unwilling to proceed because of something on the floor ahead. As Diemschutz went to get a candle, he heard a coach and horse nearing. When he returned with the candle, he discovered to his horror why his pony refused to budge. A woman with her throat slashed was blocking its path, and the blood from the murder victim was still flowing, forming a pool. With a shudder Diemschutz realized that he must have disturbed the killer, and looked about nervously.

The third murder victim was subsequently identified as Elizabeth Stride, a Swedish prostitute who was known locally as 'Long Liz' because of her height. In no time the police arrived at the murder scene and raided the Socialist Club. They made a thorough search of the club and interrogated each of its members, but the investigation was a waste of time. Jack was not among them. He was elsewhere, threading his way through the night to kill another woman, and this time he was determined to finish the job without any interruptions.

A mere forty-five minutes after the murder of 'Long Liz' Stride, the fourth victim of Jack the Ripper was found horribly mutilated in Mitre Square. Her name was

Catherine Eddowes, a 43-year-old prostitute who had been released from Bishopsgate Police Station at 1 a.m. after being detained for drunkenness. Immediately after leaving the station, she had gone off in search of a client and had walked straight into the arms of the Ripper. That morning Jack was unusually lucky. Ten minutes after he had killed Eddowes and washed his bloody hands in a communal sink nearby, a policeman walked through the square and discovered the body.

Later that morning, at 3 a.m., PC Long was walking along Goulston Street when he discovered a piece of bloodstained apron that had been cut from the Mitre Square victim's clothing. And on the wall of a nearby passageway, someone had scrawled in chalk:

> The Juwes are
> The men that
> Will not
> be Blamed
> for nothing

Police guarded the passageway until the head of the CID, Inspector MacWilliam arrived. The inspector wanted to take a photograph of the chalked message, but he needed the permission of his superior, Superintendent Arnold. But Arnold wouldn't grant him permission because he feared that the word 'Juwes' contained in the cryptic message would incite anti-Semitic riots. The Metropolitan Police commissioner, Sir Charles Warren, later turned up at the scene and washed the message off the wall claiming to share the same fear as Superintendent Arnold.

Jack the Ripper seemed to prefer working at weekends. His first murder took place on a Friday, his second on a Saturday, his third and fourth on a Sunday, and his final murder, that of 25-year-old Mary Kelly, was carried out on a Friday. But before the gruesome grand finale, the Ripper was inactive for over a month for some unknown reason. The hiatus ended on 9 November, and the Autumn of Terror resumed when a rent collector hammered on the door of 13 Miller's Court, demanding what was due to him. No answer came, so the collector carefully put his hand through a jagged hole in a window pane and pulled the curtain aside. He immediately regretted doing this, for what was revealed by the action made him dizzy with nausea. There in the dark bedroom lay the unrecognizable carcass of Mary Kelly on a blood-soaked bed. She had been skinned to the bone. Her torn-out heart rested on a pillow, and what had once been her pretty young face was now a shredded mess. It was later calculated that the Ripper must have taken at least an hour to mutilate the corpse so savagely.

In the grate the remains of a woman's clothes – the rim of a hat and pieces of a skirt – were still smouldering. These clothes did not belong to the murder victim, however, and their significance is still unknown. It is possible that the Ripper disguised himself as a woman in order to gain his victim's confidence.

After the horrible murder of Mary Kelly, Jack the Ripper retired from his satanic work. Why he suddenly stopped is hard to explain. Serial killers, driven on by bloodlust, usually keep on killing until they are captured.

Over the years many theories have deen advanced to make sense of the murders but none of them completely fits the facts. People suspected of being Jack the Ripper have included Queen Victoria's physician Sir William Gull (who was seventy-one years old at the time of the murders); the Duke of Clarence; Virginia Woolf's cousin, James Kenneth Stephen; a black magician, said to have the power of invisibility, named Robert D'Onston; and Birkenhead-born mass-murderer Frederick Deeming. In 1993 Liverpool cotton merchant James Maybrick (see

p. 77) was also named as the Ripper, and a diary, said to be written by Maybrick in the late 1880s and entitled *The Diary of Jack the Ripper* was published. The book was denounced by many dating experts as a hoax in the same mould as the 'Hitler Diaries'.

One of the little-known facts about the Ripper case is that there were two apparently genuine letters sent to the capital's police force from Liverpool during the Ripper's reign of terror. On 29 September 1888 the first letter warned: 'Beware, I shall be at work on the 1st and 2nd Inst. in Minories at twelve midnight, and I give the authorities a good chance, but there is never a policeman near me when I am at work. Yours, Jack the Ripper.'

On the following night, the Ripper was indeed 'at work', murdering the two prostitutes Stride and Eddowes. The latter was found just a stone's throw from the Minories. But the police were very amateurish in those days, and chose to ignore the warning letter, much to their later embarrassment.

A couple of days later, a second letter was sent from Liverpool to the London police. It read: 'What fools the police are. I even give them the name of the street where I am living. Yours, Jack the Ripper.'

The address referred to was 'Prince William Street, Liverpool', written at the top of the letter. The police did not make enquiries at the Toxteth street because they thought the Liverpool letters had been penned by a crackpot.

Were the letters genuine? In March 1931 a former member of the Metropolitan Police named Robert Spicer revealed to the *Daily Express* his belief that he had actually caught Jack the Ripper when he was a uniformed beat constable in his twenties. Spicer said he was on patrol in the East End in the early hours of 30 September 1888 – the night the Ripper struck twice – when he spotted a well-dressed man with a Gladstone bag chatting to a local prostitute named Rosy in a dark alleyway. As Spicer got nearer to the couple, he noticed that the man's cuffs were blood-stained. Spicer immediately confronted the man and asked him what he was doing out at that unearthly hour. The stranger seemed outraged and told the policeman that it was no business of his to ask what he was doing. Spicer took the man into custody and marched him to Commercial Street Police Station. Rosy followed closely behind them out of curiosity.

Spicer took the shady character before the station's duty inspector and proudly said that the man he'd brought in should be charged on suspicion of being the Whitechapel Murderer. But the station inspector warned the young policeman that he had no right to arrest a man who was obviously a 'respectable doctor'.

The disillusioned Spicer watched in disbelief as the doctor, who gave a Brixton address, was allowed to leave the station without explaining where the blood on his cuffs came from, and without revealing the contents of his Gladstone bag.

Spicer said he saw the doctor on several other occasions after his inexplicable release, often accosting other prostitutes in the East End area. Whenever he spotted him, Spicer would shout, 'Hello Jack! Still after them.' At this, the doctor would invariably flee.

In 1972 journalist B.E. Reilly investigated the Spicer story and systematically researched the background to every Brixton practitioner in the medical register of the late 1880s. To his great surprise, the list of suspects was narrowed down to just one candidate. This doctor had been born in India, but his family were from a northern province of England. All his life he had had connections with Liverpool, but Reilly refused to say if this meant that the doctor's family lived there. Although there were many rumours at the time of Reilly's discovery that the

Ripper suspect's family lived in Rodney Street, and that the suspect himself was buried in St James's Cemetery in December 1888. Reilly, who was investigating the Spicer story for the *Journal of the City of London Police*, found that his prime suspect's death certificate stated that he died in December 1888 from septic abcess of tubercular origin. If this is so, it would explain why the Ripper murders suddenly ceased. But what was the Ripper suspect's name? According to Reilly, the suspect's surname was very common, but for some reason he refused to divulge it.

Did Reilly hit on the truth, or is he just one of the countless Ripperologists who have vainly convinced themselves that they have unmasked history's most famous unknown murderer?

Another Liverpudlian Ripper suspect was James Kelly, who had been born in Limerick in 1860, but emigrated to Liverpool in his youth. Through the recent research of writer and amateur historian John Morrison of Leytonstone, it has been established that Sir Charles Warren apparently thought Kelly was Jack the Ripper, and an official independent inquiry behind closed doors reached the same conclusion.

After four years of delving into files from the Public Record Office and the Home Office, and scouring through electoral registers and newspaper archives, Morrison pieced together an unusual story that seems to throw light on the Ripper murders. What follows is a summary of the facts unearthed by Morrison.

In 1887 28-year-old James Kelly met a young Irish girl in Liverpool named Mary, and fell deeply in love with her. Although Kelly was already married, he threw himself into a passionate affair with the beautiful colleen and she became pregnant. Mary changed her surname to Kelly, as she was sure James would soon wed her, but was horrified when she learned that her lover was a married man. James Kelly's wife heard about her husband's affair and accused him of adultery. Kelly snapped, and after a terse brawl with his wife, he picked up a pointed table knife and stabbed her to death.

Kelly was arrested, charged with his wife's murder, and sent to the hospital wing of the Liverpool Prison, where a doctor observed him to assess his mental condition. Kelly knew he would certainly hang if the doctor found him sane, so he deliberately altered his behaviour by faking periodic fits of laughter. The ruse worked. When Kelly was tried at the Liverpool Assizes at St George's Hall, he was found 'guilty but insane' and was committed to Broadmoor Prison.

By this time Mary Kelly had left Liverpool and taken up lodgings in an Irish ghetto in East London. She bore Kelly's child and put it in the care of a local Roman Catholic convent. Rather than face grim destitution, Mary Kelly decided to descend into the seedy world of prostitution.

Around the same time in January 1888, James Kelly was ready to escape from Broadmoor. He had made himself a pass key from a metal spring. After leaving his cell and creeping down the corridors of the prison, Kelly entered an empty unlocked room, looking for clothes to hide his prisoner's uniform. There he stumbled on a strong-box. He picked the lock of the box with the spring wire and saw to his delight that it contained the wages of the prison staff in gold sovereigns. Kelly took the bag of sovereigns, then made his way into the prison yard. He climbed the wall and leapt not only to freedom but also into *The Guinness Book of Records*: Kelly was to become the longest-escaped prisoner in British criminal history – some thirty-nine years on the run.

The superintendent at Broadmoor was understandably embarrassed by Kelly's audacious robbery and escape, as was the home secretary, Henry Matthews, who promptly ordered a cover-up. None of the warders was to breathe a word of the escape to anyone, and the inmates of Broadmoor were to be told that James Kelly had been moved to another prison. Matthews summoned Sir Charles Warren to the Home Office and assigned to him the task of tracking down Kelly. The commissioner reluctantly agreed to take part in the cover-up, and promised he would do his utmost to capture the gaol-breaker.

With enough stolen money to provide Kelly and his lover with a passage to a new life in their native Ireland, the escaped prisoner made his way back to Liverpool and searched for Mary. For months he roamed the city, seeking his only reason to live, but she was nowhere to be seen. As the summer died away and the leaves began to fall, James Kelly bumped into an old friend who had just returned from the capital; what's more he had news about the elusive Mary. In total disbelief Kelly listened as his friend told him that his sweetheart had 'dropped' the baby and had gone 'on the game' in Whitechapel, East London. The bottom fell out of Kelly's world, despite the money and freedom he possessed. From that awful moment of the shocking revelation he became a changed man. Before he caught the train to London, Kelly was heard to repeat over and over: 'I'll rip her heart out!'

After his arrival in Whitechapel, James Kelly waited until nightfall before stalking the gaslit streets in search of Mary. He decided he would systematically question every prostitute in the area about Mary's whereabouts, and then kill each one he spoke to so they could not alert Mary or the police. And so Kelly questioned the first woman of the night he encountered, Mary Ann Nicholls (the Ripper's first victim), who was in a drunken state. Kelly asked her if she knew a Mary Kelly; Nicholls' reply is unknown, but Morrison says Kelly probably showed her a gold sovereign, took her into a dark alley, then killed her. Kelly's brutal *modus operandi* claimed the lives of three other prostitutes who may have each given their killer pieces of information that finally led him to 13 Miller's Court, where Mary Kelly was lodging.

According to Morrison, James Kelly must have been the unidentified man who was seen talking to Mary hours before she was killed. Indeed Mary Kelly's lover, George Hutchinson, told police he had seen Mary in the company of a young well-dressed man of around thirty years or less, which fits the escaped prisoner's description.

Morrison says that Mary would have been puzzled by her former lover's presence, as she would have been under the impression that he was still in prison. But because of the cover-up instigated by the home secretary, James Kelly could have told Mary that he'd been released from jail having been found innocent of his wife's murder.

So James Kelly lured Mary back to Miller's Court, perhaps with the promise of a share of his gold sovereigns, then savagely released all the months of bottled-up hatred by tearing apart the girl who had betrayed him and abandoned his child for a life of vice. If this happened, it would explain why, out of all the other murder victims, Mary Kelly suffered the full fury of the Ripper's knife, and it would also explain the Ripper's sudden retirement after Mary's death.

It is an intriguing story, but that's all it is, surely. Not according to Morrison, who claims he has discovered a disturbing piece of official information that may provide the solution to the greatest mystery in the history of crime.

In April 1927 James Kelly was a 67-year-old vagrant with failing health who was starting to feel the toll of sleeping on park benches, and so he finally gave himself up to the authorities. He told them that his thirty-nine years on the run had been spent in Paris and New York.

Kelly was charged with having escaped from legal custody and stealing the staff wages from Broadmoor Prison, but the weather-worn vagrant couldn't care less. After sleeping under the stars in winter for so long, he looked forward to having a decent night's leep in a comfortable bunk in Broadmoor. But he was not sent there; he was put in Dartmoor Prison, the toughest, coldest gaol in Britain.

After spending two years in the miserable, soul-destroying prison, Kelly's health worsened, and he feared he was about to die, so he confessed to being Jack the Ripper. The prison governor was intrigued by the confession and informed the home secretary, who immediately arranged a conference with the attorney general in command of the situation. After a long, drawn-out discussion Stanley Baldwin's Government was presented with Kelly's confession, together with files containing comments made by Sir Charles Warren and other police officials who had worked on the Ripper murders.

Morrison says that the Home Office of the day admitted the following, which he saw in a classified file: 'Gentlemen, it has been established, beyond a possible doubt, that a certain James Kelly, who escaped from Broadmoor Lunatic Asylum on 28th January 1888, and the infamous "Jack the Ripper", are one and the same person.'

Morrison has pointed out that the year the Home Office statement was buried away in obscure files, mainland Britain was witnessing increasing demonstrations of dissent by the so-called Irish rebels, and the Irish statesman Eamon de Valera had just founded the Fianna Fail party. It was thus hardly the time for the Home Office to admit that an Irishman had made a laughing stock of Scotland Yard and the British penal system – that would have provided the Irish rebels with propaganda on a plate.

Despite the two intriguing accounts offered by Reilly and Morrison, I still think that the true solution is much more sinister and lies undiscovered in a completely different direction. Indeed, in my opinion, the only man who knew the Ripper's real identity was Jack himself, and that he took his dreadful secret with him to the grave.

9 The Man in the Iron Tube

While clearing up rubble from the aftermath of a German air raid on Liverpool in 1943, the group of American soldiers probably regarded the long black metal tube protruding from the bottom of the bomb crater near Great Homer Street as a piece of shattered pipe. The GIs tried to dislodge the piece of 'piping' with a mechanical digger, but it wouldn't budge. In the summer of that year a second attempt was made to remove the obstruction with a more powerful mechanical digger, and this time the tubular piece of scrap was successfully uprooted.

As the dust from the difficult excavation settled, it became apparent that the metallic tube was no ordinary pipe, but a riveted sheet-iron cylinder 6 feet 9 inches in length and 18 inches in diameter. However, the sealed cylinder aroused no more than a passing interest among the soldiers who had more pressing matters to attend to, and so the tube was left among the debris of the blitzed site. There it lay forgotten until Friday 13 July 1945, when a nine-year-old boy playing on the bombed wasteland came across the unidentified relic while playing hide-and-seek with his friends. Little Tommy Lawless was hiding behind the tube when he noticed a boot poking out from a hole in one end of the cylinder. Tommy, who had never owned a pair of boots in his life, was delighted at his find, thinking that his barefoot days were over at last. He gently pulled the boot free – and saw to his horror that it had come off the foot of a skeleton. Terrified, Tommy fled from his startled playmates, and did not stop running until he saw PC Robert Baillie walking his beat in Great Homer Street. Breathlessly the youngster told the policeman what he had found, and in so doing launched the inquiry into the baffling case of the Man in the Iron Tube.

Shortly after 1 p.m. that day the cylinder and its gruesome contents were taken to the city morgue. After a detailed description of the strange artefact had been recorded, an engineer was called in to open the cylinder with an oxy-acetylene blowtorch. When the smoking tube was finally cut open, Dr Charles Harrison and the engineer looked at its occupant in total astonishment. To Harrison, senior lecturer in pathology at Liverpool University, it seemed that he was about to have the unusual task of performing a post-mortem on a body that evidently dated back to the age of Queen Victoria.

The skeleton was resplendent in a morning coat, striped narrow trousers and the fine pair of elastic-sided boots that had caught the eye of little Tommy Lawless. The position of the cadaver was strange: it lay lengthwise along the tube on a bed of sacking with its skull (which still had hair attached to it) resting on a pillow that consisted of a brick wrapped in a sack. This suggested that the man in the tube had been sleeping when he died.

Doctor Harrison's examination revealed that the body was that of a six-foot-tall middle-aged male. But that was all the doctor was able to say about the mysterious corpse. He could not explain how the man in the tube had met his death.

The police called in Dr J.B. Firth, a highly respected forensic expert from Preston. Firth's examination of the Victorian produced some intriguing results. Among the remains he discovered two diaries: one book covered July 1884 and the other contained entries for June 1884. From a pocket in the dead man's morning coat, Firth extracted a bundle of papers that were encapsulated in a revolting wax-like substance, the residue of the body's decomposed tissue. Firth skilfully applies various organic solvents to the waxen lump and with great perseverance finally managed to extricate thirteen separate documents. Most of the documents referred to a certain T.C. Williams & Co. of Leeds Street, Liverpool. A postcard among the recovered papers was also addressed to T.C. Williams.

Now that the police had a name to work with, their investigation could begin in earnest. Detective Inspector John Morris delved into the city's archives and scoured the electoral registers of the 1880s. In a business register for 1883 he came across a firm trading under the name of T.C. Williams & Co. The address was 18 to 20 Leeds Street. The firm was described in the yellowed text of the old register as 'Oil Merchants, Paint & Varnish Manufacturers'. Morris established that the head of the firm was a Mr Thomas Cregeen Williams, who lived at 29 Clifton road, Anfield. Moreover, the inspector discovered that in the following year the financial affairs of the plant works were for some reason being investigated by a firm of accountants. What became of the company after that is a mystery, for there is no further reference to the business in any of the Liverpool trade directories after 1884.

Inspector Morris searched the local registers for some record of the death of Thomas Cregeen Williams, but he could find none. Morris hypothesized that Mr Williams had hidden himself from his creditors by crawling into the metal tube and had died from accidental asphyxiation. But it is an unsatisfactory theory. In the 1880s it was more usual for debtors simply to board a ship and work their passage abroad when their creditors got too close.

Firth's examination of the Man in the Iron Tube also reached a dead end. The forensic expert analysed the clothes and bones of the corpse for traces of poison but could find none. So what are we to make of the unknown man? How did he come to die in his cylindrical coffin? Was he murdered? Or was he a murderer hiding from justice? The questions remain unanswered.

10　The Rainhill Psychopath

What is a psychopath? According to the accepted textbook definition, it is a person who behaves violently or antisocially and shows no guilt or feelings for others. This does not mean that the psychopath exhibits these traits all the time; otherwise he or she would be easily recognizable as such. From the data we have on psychopaths, it is evident that the majority lead largely ordinary lives until some mental disturbance triggers a drastic personality change.

Another question: is there a dormant psychopath in all of us? Many familiar idiomatic phrases in the English language seem to indicate that we acknowledge a dark and dangerous force deep in the human mind that surfaces and takes control of the ego. We have all heard or used phrases such as, 'I don't know what came over me'; 'I must have been out of my mind'; 'I must have been mad'; or, 'He can't have been himself when he did that.' Another expression along these lines is 'I don't know what possessed me' – a throwback to medieval times, when possession by demons was sometimes cited as the cause of a bad deed. Of course, since the work of Freud and other psychiatrists, demonic possession has been explained away as a mundane personality disorder, but even with all the latest technological marvels at the psychoanalyst's disposal, the mechanisms of the mind are still shrouded in mystery.

So the honest answer to the original question concerning the nature of the psychopath is that nobody knows, and, very often, nobody knows until it is too late. Take the case of Frederick Bailey Deeming, a seemingly normal, good-looking young man with captivating blue eyes, wavy sandy hair, who loved to shower the opposite sex with gifts. But behind the charming persona there lurked a callous killer.

Frederick Deeming was born in Birkenhead in 1853, the youngest of a poverty-stricken family of seven children. In his teens he abandoned his home for a life at sea, working as a ship's steward. He travelled the world, and for some reason began to adopt several aliases such as Lawson, Duncan, Druin and Williams, to name but a few. On his voyages around the globe he was alleged to have stopped off in various countries to perpetrate a series of murders and frauds. On several occasions he was rumoured to have entered into marriage for financial gain, and always ended up killing his spouse before making off with the proceeds. There were also claims that Deeming once knifed a Zulu to death over some dispute in the South African Cape. On another occasion, he was said to have shot thirteen lions in a single day to satisfy the incredible bloodlust he was developing.

When the black-hearted seafarer gave up his occupation and returned home, he found employment as a plumber and gas-fitter and also found himself a pretty young girl called Marie James, who instantly fell for his good looks and married him. Marie bore him four children, but Deeming later callously abandoned his wife and offspring, and went across the Mersey to seek a new life and a new love.

In July 1891 Deeming took out a lease on a cottage called Dinham Villa at Rainhill, near St Helens, where he posed as an army inspector named Albert Williams who was suposedly acting on behalf of a Colonel Brooks. It wasn't long before Emily Mather, the landlady's 25-year-old daughter, took an admiring interest in dashing Deeming, and suddenly romance was in the air. Pretty young Emily was enthralled by Deeming's tales of his seafaring days. At last she had met her ideal man ...

One day Deeming's abandoned wife and family turned up unannounced at the villa. With amazing calm, Deeming casually passed off Marie as his sister. Infatuated Emily believed the tale, and Deeming realized that drastic action was now needed to give some credibility to his story. Marie and the children had to be disposed of. First he went out to buy a pickaxe and several bags of cement, then prepared to wait for the right moment. This came soon enough; during the night, when his wife and four children were sleeping peacefully in their beds. Then he went to work. In his nightshirt Deeming crept into their bedrooms and systematically began slitting their throats, though inexplicably he chose to strangle one of his daughters.

The next task he performed was the entombment of the bodies. He hid the five corpses in the shallow graves he had created under the hearthstones of the kitchen floor, and later employed labourers to assist him in cementing over the kitchen's uneven flags. Deeming carried this off by explaining that Colonel Brooks hated uneven floors. Unknowingly, then, the labourers helped to entomb the only obstacles that had stood in the way of Deeming's romance with Miss Mather. When the newly surfaced kitchen floor had finally dried, Deeming threw a party to which he invited his sweetheart Emily and several other guests. During the merrymaking, Deeming danced with the unsuspecting guests upon the graves of his wife and children. Later that evening Deeming proposed to Emily Mather, who, with a slight blush, accepted. The couple were married at St Anne's Church, Rainhill, on 22 September 1891.

Shortly after the marriage Deeming became uneasy about living at Dinham Villa, fearing that his slowly decomposing victims might start to smell. He told Emily that he needed to vacate the house because 'the Colonel' had decided to occupy it after all. Deeming left Dinham Villa and for a short while moved into his new wife's home half a mile away. But he started to get itchy feet again and told Emily that as an inspector of regiments, he had received correspondence from the British Army requesting him to be stationed in Windsor, Australia.

On 15 December Deeming and his wife arrived in Melbourne and travelled out to the city's surburban district of Windsor, where they found suitable accommodation at 57 Andrew Street, which was a rented cottage. The couple unpacked their bags, with Emily feeling quite content about her new life Down Under. Already, however, Deeming was planning the next move in his infamous career. Nine days later, on Christmas Eve, he took an axe and brought it down six times on Emily's head. Then to make sure she was finished, he cut her throat. Up came the hearthstone which was to become Emily's headstone.

Early in the following year Deeming packed his bags again and boarded a Sydney-bound steamer. On board ship he met a beautiful young woman named Kate Rounsefell, and before the steamer had reached Sydney Harbour Deeming had won her heart. He proposed and offered her an impressive diamond ring. Kate, complaining of an excess of haste, turned him down; nevertheless she decided she wanted to get to know him. Deeming told her he was going to join the goldrush in Western Australia, and that he would soon be a very wealthy man. Still, Kate was not sure about marriage, but said she would follow him.

Meanwhile, back in Melbourne, a woman was enquiring about the vacant house at 57 Andrew Street. The landlord of the premises accompanied the woman to the address and allowed her to inspect the place. In the bedroom the landlord and the prospective tenant encountered the terrible stench of Emily's rotting corpse. The unscrupulous landlord claimed the smell was merely from dead mice, but the woman left, feeling nauseous. With the help of another man, the landlord lifted up the hearthstone in the bedroom, and the aroma of decaying tissue suddenly became stronger. The police were informed, and when they later broke up a layer of cement under the bedroom floor, they discovered a hollowed-out grave containing the doubled-up body of a woman. Police inquiries determined that the name of the house of horror's last tenant was a 'Mr Druin', who had mysteriously left without giving any notice. During a thorough search of the house, the police found a luggage ticket which they traced to a shipping clerk. He recalled booking a sea passage for a man who called himself 'Baron Swanston'.

The police in Melbourne lost no time in cabling the information to their colleagues in Perth. There Detective George Gurney made further enquiries, and discovered that a 'Baron Swanston' had stayed at the city's Shamrock Hotel and furthermore had left a forwarding address – a house at Southern Cross in the Western Australian outback. Detective Gurney quickly tele-graphed the police outpost at Southern Cross, and the following morning, two armed police constables rode to Fraser's Gold Mine and arrested Deeming. He reacted with outraged innocence, protesting, 'This is all a mistake!'

Deeming was bundled into a mail coach and the 200 mile journey to Perth commenced. During the journey to justice, news broke of the horrendous discovery of

Deeming's butchered family at Dinham Villa in Rainhill, England. Shortly afterwards Kate Rounsefell, who was on her way to meet her fiancé received a telegram from her sister warning her not to go further. Kate almost fainted when she realized how close she had come to a horrible death.

While awaiting trial Deeming spent most of his time making morbid sketches of gallows and reading from the Bible. Then a rumour circulated the prison alleging that Deeming had confessed to being Jack the Ripper. Despite the fact that Deeming was not even in London at the time of the Whitechapel murders, the newspapers had a field day, and the *Melbourne Evening Standard* soon ran the sensational headline: JACK THE RIPPER: DEEMING AT ALDGATE ON THE NIGHT OF THE WHITECHAPEL MURDERS.

The Murder trial opened on 8 May 1892 at Melbourne Criminal Court. Deeming, referred to in court as Albert O. Williams, was tried for killing his wife Emily, but he had not been charged with the Rainhill murders. His defence counsel was a young barrister named Alfred Deakin, who later became Australia's prime minister three times. Deakin argued that Deeming was insane, and so could not be held repsonsible for his actions. But the rhetoric was useless. On the final day of the trial Deeming obtained the court's permission to address the jury, and for a whole hour, he maintained that he had not been given a fair trial, as the newspaper had already made up people's minds for them.

After thirty minutes of deliberation, the jury returned a guilty verdict.

On the sunny morning of 23 May 1892 Frederick Deeming walked to the scaffold smoking a large cigar giving to him by the hangman. By now his hair had turned white. By a dark coincidence, the name of the gaol where Deeming was to be despatched was Swanston – as in 'Baron Swanston', one of his aliases. Outside the walls of the gaol, a crowd of 12,000 had gathered to be the first to hear the news of the execution.

Deeming was strapped up and his hands were bound together. His face was covered with the white cap, and the hangman deftly secured the noose around his neck. Seconds before the lever was pulled, Deeming was heard to whisper, 'Lord receive my spirit.'

11   The Stadium Steps Murder

During September 1960 Valerie Sellers, an attractive 19-year-old waitress from Gronant, Flintshire, proudly introduced her boyfriend to her parents. Her sweetheart was John Christopher McMenemy, a 23-year-old Liverpudlian with red hair and a rather pallid complexion. The young man asked Valerie's father, Isaac, for permission to marry his daughter and, after much deliberation, Mr Sellers gave his consent. The couple suffered a few ups and downs, however, and their wedding plans were postponed. Then, on 30 July 1961, while McMenemy was staying at Valerie's home, Mr Sellers confronted the young man and asked him if he really had any intentions of marrying his daughter. McMenemy said he had, and Valerie told her father she would like to marry her boyfriend. But half an hour afterwards McMenemy suddenly told Valerie: 'I never will – marry you.'

Mr Sellers assured his heartbroken daughter that McMenemy's decision was for the best as he was unemployed and would therefore be unable to maintain her.

Before he went to bed that night, Mr Sellers gave McMenemy half-a-crown (12½p) to pay for his bus fare home, and McMenemy left the house.

On 12 August, he returned to the Sellers' home to repay the £3 and ten shillings (£3.50) he owed Valerie's father. Mr Sellers took the money and bluntly told McMenemy he was no longer welcome at the house and advised him to return to his hometown. McMenemy left in a huff.

On his way to bed at around midnight Mr Sellers looked into his daughter's bedroom and saw her sleeping. But at 5.30 a.m., when he went to wake her for work, Valerie's bed was empty. He suspected the obvious: his daughter had sneaked out of the house in the early hours to rejoin her barred lover. What Mr Sellers did not know at this point was that he would never see his pretty young daughter alive again.

Five days after the moonlight flit Valerie and McMenemy turned up in Warrington, where they managed to hitch a ride up to Glasgow in the car of a Mr Edward O'Sullivan. At the end of the journey McMenemy secretly produced a sheath knife and hid it under the car's dashboard without the driver's knowing. After a short stay in Scotland, Mr O'Sullivan took McMenemy and Valerie to Liverpool. As McMenemy left the car, he put his hand under the dashboard and, this time in full view of the driver, retrieved the knife he had secreted there. O'Sullivan was naturally uneasy about McMenemy's intimidating behaviour, and was only too glad to see the back of the hitch-hikers.

On the following morning on Sunday 20 August, at around 1.40 a.m., two policeman walking down Bixteth Street, towards Tithebarn Street in Liverpool city centre, observed a couple, whom they later learned to be McMenemy and Valerie, with their arms around one another, walking up the street towards the Liverpool Stadium, the city's famous boxing venue, situated off Old Hall Street. The officers noticed that Valerie seemed to be crying.

At precisely 3.48 a.m. John McMenemy entered a telephone call box at the Pier Head and dialled 100.

'Which number do you require?' the operator asked.

McMenemy paused, the told the operator to take a message. He said that there was a body at the top of the steps of the Liverpool Stadium.

'Where are you speaking from?' said the operator.

McMenemy hung up, then strolled to a waterfront refreshment stall where he chain-smoked and drank cup after cup of coffee. The police, meanwhile, were working with the Post Office to trace the night caller, and within a matter of minutes a wireless message was transmitted to Constables Smith and Walton, who were on motor-patrol duty near to the scene of the reported crime.

Shortly before 4 a.m. their Land Rover pulled up at the stadium and the two officers ran to the building's main entrance. On the steps they found the heavily bloodstained body of Valerie Sellers lying with a raincoat draped across her. Near to her head was an unusual clue: a man's tie. One of the officers lifted the raincoat and saw that the young woman had obviously died from multiple stab wounds to her chest and stomach. There were fourteen wounds in all. Liverpool Stadium, world-renowned temple of the noble art, now resembled a Mayan sacrificial altar.

The police and the Post Office were remarkably swift in narrowing down the source of the telephone call, and a matter of minutes after the discovery of the body Smith, Walton and another police officer arrived at the Pier Head. McMenemy had been waiting for them, and before the policemen spotted him, he slipped away from the coffee stall and hurled the silver coins and the pound note he had taken from Valerie's purse into the River Mersey.

The three policemen approached McMenemy, and one of them instantly noticed that the young man was not wearing a tie. Constable Smith said that he was making enquiries into the very recent murder of a young woman and asked McMenemy if he could account for his movements during the past hour.

'I've been walking about,' was all that McMenemy could offer by way of an alibi.

During the questioning an officer noticed the bloodstain on the cuff of McMenemy's right sleeve, as well as a reddish stain on his right hand. As the suspect was being taken to the rear of the coffee stall for further interrogation, McMenemy suddenly said: 'It's in my back. In my waist band.'

From McMenemy's belt one of the officers withdrew a sheath knife, positioned at the base of his back.

McMenemy then said, morosely, 'She was my girlfriend. I stabbed her once and she groaned so I kept on to put her out of her misery.'

Constable Smith cautioned McMenemy and he was taken to the bridewell, where he was again searched and interviewed at length by Detective Inspector Wade. The search yielded three articles which had belonged to the dead girl: a cigarette lighter, a purse and a bracelet engraved with the words 'Chris and Val' ('Chris' referred to the middle name by which McMenemy chose to be known.) During the interview with Inspector Wade, McMenemy made a full confession and revealed how a petty row over money had cost Valerie Sellers her life.

He explained: 'She would not give me the money. So I stabbed her, but when she started gurgling I decided to finish her off. It is my fault. I want everyone to know what happened.'

In chilling detail his statement went on:

First, I did not mean to kill her, but when she was arguing about the flat I told her I wanted some money and I was going to get some rum and go away. She would not give it to me, and said, 'You can have your own, but you are not having mine.'

I said, 'I am having it!' and grabbed her purse. She grabbed it back. I had my knife in my hand. I had been cutting a match. I told her if she did not give me the purse I would stick the knife in her. She said she would not give it to me, so I stuck the knife in her stomach and grabbed the purse. She grabbed my hand and was holding the knife. We fell down the stairs, struggling. She was calling my name. I stabbed her a few more times. I pulled my tie off with the other hand and put it round her throat, knowing that she was dead. I laid her down on the floor. That's all there is. I went around buying coffee and cigarettes out of the money in her purse. She had just under £3. First I was going to make a run for it, but I got thinking about her so I went down to the Pier Head and walked around, thinking, and I realised it was hopeless to run.'

Four days after the murder Mr Sellers was taken to the city mortuary to identify the body of his daughter.

Home Office pathologist Doctor Charles Arthur St Hill carried out the post-mortem examination of the murder victim and recorded the cause of death. Miss Sellers had died from multiple stab wounds. The attack had been so ferocious that four ribs had been severed; one wound to the stomach was 5½ inches deep.

The pathologist also revealed that Valerie had been two months pregnant when she died.

John Christopher McMenemy was tried at Liverpool Crown Court on Wednesday 1 November 1961. He did not give evidence and no witnesses were called in his defence. His counsel, Mr J.S. Watson Q.C., referring to the fatal quarrel, said McMenemy 'may have taken some of her property ... But,' he argued, 'these two people were in love. They wanted to marry each other. Persons in love regard each other's property as their own.'

Lord Chief Justice Parker reminded the jury, however, that the capital charge was of murdering Miss Sellers in furtherance of theft.'

McMenemy was found guilty and sentenced to death. The date of his execution was set for 22 November, but on 18 November the case was heard by the Court of Criminal Appeal. Mr Watson, again representing McMenemy, asked the court to substitute a verdict of manslaughter on the grounds of diminished responsibility. The appeal was dismissed and 8 December became the new execution date; but on 24 November a reprieve was recommended by the home secretary, and the death sentence was commuted to life imprisonment.

12   A Shooting at the Station

Unsolved crimes always fascinate the public. When the professionals can find no solution to account for some lethal deed, the armchair detectives take a delight in propounding their own theories. The following incident, which occurred over sixty years ago, is still unsolved, although many detectives, including the amateur variety, have attempted to piece together the events – the events that led to the tragic shooting of two men in a Cheshire police station.

In April 1929, the Reverend Frank Hayward left his church near Oldham in order to visit his parents in Runcorn. His fiancée, herself the daughter of a parson, accompanied him on the trip.

Frank's father, Charles Hayward, a superintendent in the Cheshire Constabulary, was very proud of his only son and had sacrificed a great deal so that Frank could take holy orders. Frank was the apple of his father's eye, and the superintendent often said that life would be unbearable without a son to take interest in.

On this particular visit Frank told his devoted father that he planned to marry soon and had ambitions to build a new church in the not-too-distant future. Mr Hayward listened keenly to his son's aspirations, full of admiration.

On this fateful weekend Superintendent Hayward was visiting Runcorn Police Station and descended into a basement store-room accompanied by the acting sergeant on duty. The store-room contained a number of high-powered rifles, ten revolvers and 397 rounds of ammunition. This hardware had been surrendered to officers over the years, but the firearms were not used by the police. Thinking that some of the hardware in the store-room might interest his son, the superintendent decided to arrange for him to visit the station. At noon he and Frank went down into the store-room. About ten minutes later Acting Sergeant Bell, who was busy working in the station office, was startled by a loud bang. Shortly afterwards Bell heard the superintendent's voice shouting for him, and he raced down the stairs to the store-room, where he met his superior officer.

'Bell,' said Superintendent Hayward, 'something terrible has happened. My son picked up the revolver. He did not know there was anything in it, and it went off before I knew what had happened.'

Sergeant Bell ran back upstairs to phone for medical help, and on his way he heard another gunshot. Rushing back to the store-room he found the superintendent lying dead with a bullet wound in his head, just above his right ear.

The doctor arrived minutes later to find the reverend, who had a gaping bullet hole three inches above his right eye, at the point of death.

People who knew the father and son were convinced that the shooting was not the result of a murder and suicide by the father, nor suicide of the son, followed by the father. In fact Inspector Postons, one of the last people to see Frank Hayward before his death, said the young man had cheerfully told him about his forthcoming marriage and his plans to set up a new parish.

At the inquest into the double tragedy the coroner

asked Inspector Postons if anything had been troubling Superintendent Hayward prior to the shooting.

'No, sir. He was of a very cheerful disposition and he was devoted to his son,' replied the inspector.

However, some baffling details emerged at the inquest. A police constable who had cleaned all the firearms in the store-room three weeks earlier said the revolver that had killed Superintendent Hayward and his son was definitely unloaded. The officer remembered checking it and tying a box of ammunition to the firearm with string. At the inquest the constable said that anyone handling the revolver would have had to untie this string. A cursory inspection revealed that the box of ammunition had been torn open at one corner, and that two rounds were missing.

So what happened on that fateful Saturday? The bullet that killed Frank Hayward had entered his head at an angle from above, and the muzzle of the revolver had been in close proximity to the victim when fired, probably around six inches from the head. These facts seemed to indicate that Frank had been stooping when he was shot, which made the suicide and accidental death theories seem unlikely. The superintendent had told Sergeant Bell that his son had received the fatal wound after picking up the gun, yet the facts indicated that Frank was stooping when he was shot.

There was no doubt about the cause of the superintendent's death. He had shot himself, and this act of suicide was thought to have been triggered by shock he had experienced at witnessing the death of his own son.

If a murder and a suicide did take place, what was the motive? In all the dialogue of devotion uttered about his son, Superintendent Hayward made virtually no mention of Mrs Hayward, and some thought that this indicated that the superintendent's marriage was a disharmonious one. The policeman's oft-repeated remark about life being unbearable without his son does not say much for his relationship with his wife. But even so, why on earth would a devoted father suddenly decide to kill his own son in cold blood?

13   *Until You Are Dead*

On the evening of 11 August 1873 a 29-year-old Liverpool boxer by the name of James O'Connor left Cambridge Music Hall at Mill Street in the south end of the city. The concert had ended and as the audience spilled out on to the streets, O'Connor noticed an attractive woman emerging from the hall. On an impulse he asked her to accompany him to a public house to have a drink and an intimate chat. The woman, whose name was Mary Fortune, was married and, politely rejecting O'Connor's advances, walked on into the night. O'Connor followed her down the street and suddenly accused the woman of having had some money from him. The embarrassed woman turned around and started arguing with O'Connor, whereupon the boxer suddenly struck the woman in the face twice; the force of the second blow knocked her to the ground. Two passers-by on the opposite pavement witnessed the assault, and one of them, James Gaffney, ran across the road and asked O'Connor why he had hit the woman. O'Connor made no reply, but reached into the inside pocket of his jacket and produced a clasp knife. Before Gaffney could raise his arm to defend himself, O'Connor thrust the knife into his neck. Gaffney's friend, a man by the name of Metcalf, ran over the road and tackled O'Connor. Metcalf delivered a straight punch to O'Connor's jaw that sent the boxer to the floor; however, being well versed in pugilism, O'Connor was quick to recover, and he got back to his feet and plunged the knife into Metcalf's torso.

Gaffney and Metcalf were taken to the Southern Hospital. Metcalf recovered, but Gaffney's internal bleeding could not be stopped, and he died the following morning.

After taking statements from Metcalf and Mary Fortune, the police were swift in tracking down O'Connor, who was a well-known trouble-maker with a fondness for blades. He was arrested and charged with the murder of Gaffney and the attempted murder of his friend Metcalf. Before Judge Brett at the Assizes at St George's Hall, O'Connor was found guilty of both charges. He was sentenced to hang at Kirkdale Gaol early in September. O'Connor resigned himself to his fate, but he could not have imagined the mental torture that he would have to endure before his demise.

At 8 a.m. on the Monday morning of the execution the public executioner, an experienced man by the name of Calcraft, who had hanged thousands in his career and supervised several mass-hangings at Tyburn, took O'Connor and a priest on to the scaffold in the corner of the prison yard and led the condemned on to the trapdoors. O'Connor stood there smiling and shivering in the freezing morning air before six pressmen as the priest, Father Bronte, prayed. Before the white cap was put on O'Connor's head, Father Bronte offered the condemned man a crucifix to kiss, which O'Connor did with devotion. Calcraft put the noose around O'Connor's neck and drew it tight, then bound his wrists and legs with thick leather straps. Father Bronte then started to recite another prayer, and there was a crash, as Calcraft drew the bolt. O'Connor fell to what would have been a sure death — but the rope had snapped. O'Connor wriggled about in the pit below the scaffold and screamed in pain. Being bound, and blinded by the hood, he was confused to say the least, and for a moment he thought he had gone over to the other side. Father Bronte jumped down into the pit with one of the reporters. The cleric pulled back the hood from O'Connor's head and tried to console him as he loosened the noose from his rope-burned neck.

O'Connor ignored the priest and turned to the pressman with tears in his eyes, saying, 'I stood it bravely didn't I? You'll let me go off now, won't you?'

The priest bowed his head and almost started to cry as he patted O'Connor on the shoulder.

The journalist gave no answer, but scribbled O'Connor's desperate words in his notebook.

'What do you call this?' screamed O'Connor hysterically, half-realizing that he would not be 'let off'. 'Do you call this murder?' he went on, and broke down, sobbing.

As Calcraft went to get another rope, Father Bronte tried to draw O'Connor's attention to an extract from the book of Devotions, but O'Connor started ranting, 'I have not got over the pain! Lord have mercy upon me!'

The pressman jotted a few more notes and left the pit knowing that the half-hanged man would make a second drop, because the law was specific and absolute on the matter: 'There to be hanged by the neck *until you are dead*.' And the law was to be obeyed.

Within minutes James O'Connor found himself standing on the trapdoors with a noose of new rope about his neck, and the second time around the condemned had adopted such a defeatist attitude that Calcraft allowed him to adjust the noose himself and pull the white cap over his face.

Seconds before the bolt was drawn, O'Connor stood there with his head bowed. When he fell for the second time, O'Connor took eight minutes to die, because

Calcraft had made a gross error in calculating the length of the rope. He had only allowed for a drop of eight inches. Because of this second serious blunder, the hangman was never asked to despatch again at Kirkdale Gaol.

14 The Body in the Sack

At 6 p.m. on the evening of 10 December 1913 a little shop at 86 Old Hall Street was closing for the day, and the staff were getting prepared to make their journeys home. The sign above the shop read: J.C. BRADFIELD & CO.

Tarpaulin manufacturer John Copeland Bradfield owned the shop, but he wasn't a man who liked to be stuck behind a counter all day; so he let his spinster sister, Christina, take care of that side of the business, while he spent most of his time supervizing the industrial processes at the factory he owned in Great Howard Street.

Christina Bradfield was a priggish, but rather attractive woman of forty – although she looked much younger – and a very concientious manageress. Her staff of three were Miss Margaret Venables, the 21-year-old typist and secretary; George Sumner, a 20-year-old assistant and packer, and Samuel Elltoft, the 18-year-old shop-boy. Samuel did a little bit of everything, including helping to organize the chaotic mounds of horse-cloths and rope that accumulated in the stores.

Shortly after 6.10 p.m. Miss Venables put on her hat and coat, and hurried out of the shop to catch her train home. Miss Bradfield was counting the day's takings, while George Sumner was sweeping the shop floor, all the while glancing furtively at his female boss. Whether he was lusting after her or the takings is hard to say. But as she counted the golden sovereigns and the silver florins and ordered them into neat columns, he moved in closer to her, still sweeping, still undecided as to what he wanted. Meanwhile, his 18-year-old workmate was putting up the shutters outside. It is not known if he saw the vile act that took place that night.

Inside the shop, Sumner finally snapped. Without warning, he threw down his broom and began to rip the clothes off Miss Bradfield, while sexually assaulting her. She screamed, and Sumner responded by picking up a circular pin of hard wood which was used for splicing rope, and he beat her head repeatedly with it until she was silent. Sumner stood over the battered, half-naked corpse, and realized the enormity of his crime. He now had to dispose of the evidence. He instructed Elltoft to help him haul the body into a sack, and probably either reminded the teenager that he could be charged with being an accessory after the fact, or simply promised that his assistance would be rewarded with a sum from the takings.

The two men doubled-up the blood-spattered corpse and secured its position with a rope, before easing it into a sack. Elltoft then sewed up the sack, and over an hour later, George Sumner decided it was time to get the body off of the premises. He had a plan: put the body on a cart and dump it in the Leeds & Liverpool Canal, which was only about half a mile from the shop. As Sumner was thinking about the disposal plan, there was a loud noise outside. The two terrified young men stood stock still, gaping at one another. Then Elltoft gave a sigh of relief as he realized that the gale-force winds outside had blown a shutter off the shop window. He went outside to retrieve it, and encountered an angry young man who was examining a dented bowler hat. The man was Walter

Eaves, a ship's steward on shore-leave who had recently disembarked the ivory-hulled *Empress of Britain* at the Pier Head. He had been patiently walking up and down Old Hall Street waiting for his girl to turn up.

Elltoft ignored Eaves and put the shutter back on the shop window.

'Hey! Just a minute! Your shutter's ruined my new hat,' said Eaves, pointing to the dent in his new bowler.

Elltoft scarpered into the shop to tell Sumner what had happened. A few moments later Sumner came to the door with Elltoft and quickly expresed an apology before giving Eaves a florin as compensation. As Eaves walked away, Sumner bid him goodnight and closed the door. They thought they had got rid of a potential witness. But Eaves continued to pace up and down the street, waiting for his date to arrive.

Shortly afterwards Eaves heard a trundling noise, and glanced around to see Elltoft pushing a handcart up the street, followed by Sumner. As it passed under the yellowish gaslight of a streetlamp Eaves noticed the cart was supporting a suspicious-looking sack. The young steward watched as the vehicle turned right at the top of the road and disappeared into Leeds Street. He thought about the possibility of a body being in the sack, then dismissed the gruesome thought from his imagination. Eaves glanced at his watch and resumed his pacing.

Elltoft pushed the cart down Pall Mall, which was deserted, and past empty warehouses, where the gales from the Irish Sea whined and howled like a band of grieving banshees. The tumbling cart rolled on down the length of Love Lane and across a stretch of wasteland until it finally halted by the locks of the Leeds & Liverpool Canal. Here the murderer and his accomplice got hold of each end of the sack, and, after looking around once more to make sure there were no witnesses, they tossed the body into the freezing black waters of the canal. The shrieking winds made the splash inaudible.

Sumner and Elltoft then wheeled the cart back to the shop. That was that: by tomorrow, they believed, the corpse would be lost forever in the depths of the River Mersey — but they thought wrong. Despite all the measures that a killer can take to dispose of his victim, sometimes Murphy's Law (which states that if something can go wrong, it will) rears its head. On such occasions Launcelot Gobbo's remark in *The Merchant of Venice*, that 'Truth will come to light; murder cannot be hid long', begins to ring true. And this was so in the case of the Body in the Sack. As it turned out, the body did not drift out of the canal and into the sea as was intended, but was caught up in one of the canal's lock gates, where it was discovered the following day at noon by Francis Robinson, the master of a barge. He initially thought the obstruction in the mechanism of number 3 lock was a sack of foodstuff from one of the nearby warehouses, but after pulling the sack free with a boat-hook, Robinson recoiled with horror when he noticed a black-stockinged leg dangling out of the bag.

Back at the shop in Old Hall Street, Miss Venables and Mr John Bradfield were becoming more and more concerned about the missing manageress. George Sumner and Samuel Elltoft made the occasional amateurish attempt at feigning concern, too, before lapsing back into their calm and collected moods. Later that day, the police informed Bradfield of the macabre find, and shortly afterwards he identified his sister's body at the Prince's Dock Mortuary.

It didn't take the police long to start putting two and two together, and in the early hours of the following morning at 1.30 a.m., they called at Elltoft's house in Windermere Street, Anfield, and arrested him. They also went to Sumner's residence in Boundary Lane off West Derby Road, but the murderer had already disappeared in a moonlight flit.

A manhunt was launched and every available policeman combed the streets of Liverpool for Sumner. Every dockland warehouse was thoroughly searched, as was every public house and boarding house. The fugitive's face was projected on to the screens of every cinema in the city, and a £50 reward was offered for information leading to his capture. An irresponsible rumour-monger claimed the wanted man was a stowaway on the New York-bound *Majestic*, and so the police boarded the ship and checked out all the passengers and crew. By a freak of coincidence, the ship's steward shared the same name as George Sumner, but he was not the one the police were looking for.

Back in Liverpool the police discovered that the murderer had been using an alias. His real surname was Ball. This new piece of evidence did not make the search any more successful, however. It seemed as if the murderer of Miss Bradfield had vanished off the face of the earth. But events suddenly took a positive turn on 20 December, when George Ball was finally spotted – not by a policeman but by an old schoolfriend. Ball had shaved his eyebrows, and was wearing an eye-patch and cheap spectacles at the time, but still his old friend recognized him, and followed the killer into the Mersey Lodging House Company's establishment at 84 St James's Street. The police were informed of Ball's whereabouts, and they arrested him shortly before midnight.

The murder trial opened at St George's Hall on 2 February 1914. The defence Ball offered was a ludicrous yarn about a stranger who appeared in the shop and held him at gunpoint before clubbing Miss Bradfield to death and running off with the takings. Faced with the grim fact of having a bludgeoned corpse on their hands, the two men had no alternative but to throw the body in the canal, as they knew no one would believe their story.

Then Elltoft went into the witness-box and gave a

different fictional account of that night's events. Then came the damning testimony of Walter Eaves, the steward who had been pacing Old Hall Street on the night of the murder and who had witnessed the two young men carting away the sack that had aroused his curiosity.

At the end of the trial, the jury brought in a verdict of guilty.

Ball was sentence to death. Elltoft, who was found guilty of being an accessory after the fact, was given an unprecedented lenient sentence considering the hideous nature of the crime. He was sentenced to four years' penal servitude.

15   The Pyre in the Alley

Julie Ann Christian was a 26-year-old Liverpool woman who was devoted to her family and her 30-year-old common-law husband, a former Post Office worker named Ian Thomas. The eldest of four girls, Julie was a caring, gentle and rather shy individual who spent most of her free time at her home in Teilo Street, Toxteth, with Ian, three cats and two dogs. When she wasn't attending college, where she had enrolled on a jewellery design course, she sometimes played the guitar or listened to old Beatles records. Paul McCartney was her idol.

Although Julie's parents had been divorced for twelve years, they were still friends. Julie often visited her mother's home in Aigburth every Thursday night, and every Wednesday her father Harry Christian, a government training scheme instructor who had divorced and remarried, would travel from his home in Buckley, North Wales, to see his eldest daughter.

At the age of fifteen Julie was injured in a motorcycle accident and was in traction for nearly five months. After the accident she became timid and started to lose her self-confidence. In the early 1980s she met Ian Thomas, a bright young man who had left school with ten O levels and secured a job serving behind the counter of the local post office. At seventeen Julie left home to live with him. After almost ten years of cohabitation Julie and Ian's love for one another was as strong as ever, and every time the couple went out together they would be holding hands. Upon seeing the devoted couple, the neighbours would often joke: 'Look at the lovers.'

Julie and Ian's terraced home in Teilo Street, where they had lived for five years, was spick and span inside and out, thanks to Julie's conscientious efforts, and neighbours would often comment on the house-proud couple's immaculate dwelling. But in the autumn of 1990 the house in Teilo Street became the subject of comments of a much less benign nature.

Around 3 a.m. on the Sunday morning of 11 November 1990 a neighbour living two doors away from Julie Christian awoke to the sound of someone shuffling along the back alley, dragging something. A few seconds later the dog of another neighbour started to bark furiously at the unseen alley prowler. After a few moments the noise subsided into deadly silence.

Later that day Ian Thomas took a bus ride to a do-it-yourself store in Speke where he bought the paint he would need to do a decorating job for Julie's grandmother. When he returned to Teilo Street in the evening Thomas walked over two miles to the home of Julie's mother, Pat, via the longest possible route. He could have telephoned Pat, but for some reason decided not to. When he reached Pat's home in Aigburth, he told her of his concern for Julie, who should have returned home by now. He said he had last seen Julie at 2 p.m. and that she had told him she was going to visit her sister Sally. Thomas then added that he had not had a row or anything, and could not explain Julie's absence. A few hours later Julie's sister, Sally, became extremely upset and started to cry. She told her mother that she had experienced a terrible premonition of Julie's fate. 'I have got a horrible feeling that something awful has happened to her,' she said, sobbing. When the family later went on a desperate search around the streets of south Liverpool, Sally and her sister Caroline inspected the alleyway behind Julie's home at around 1.30 a.m., and detected a strange burning smell coming from somewhere among the many black plastic bin bags dotted down the alley. Sally dismissed the smell as smoke. Children were always setting light to rubbish in the alley.

The following morning Julie Christian was still nowhere to be seen, so Thomas decided to report her disappearance to the police. Julie's dad accompanied Thomas to Admiral Street Police Station, where the young man gave a detailed description of Julie so that an officer could file a missing person's report. As Ian Thomas described the dressing-gown he had last seen Julie wearing, Mr Christian gave him a comforting pat on the back.

The police helicopter was launched and specialist search teams from the Operational Support Division were drafted into the Teilo Street area. But it was not the high-powered police search that discovered Julie Christian, but a 93-year-old man who was trying to remove piles of dumped rubbish bags from the backyard door of his house in Teilo Street on the Wednesday afternoon of November 14. As the old man pulled the smouldering bags from the door, he recoiled in horror as he saw Julie's badly-charred and unrecognizable body lying in the smouldering fire of rubbish just forty yards from her home.

A comparison of dental records was the only way of identifying the body, and once police knew beyond a doubt that the body on the makeshift pyre was Julie's, they launched a murder hunt headed by Detective Chief Inspector Tony Bennet. It was Bennet who had to break the terrible news to Harry Christian. Julie's father had been waiting at his former wife's home hoping to hear something positive about the whereabouts of his missing daughter when Bennet called. On that black day Harry opened the door, and before the policeman could speak, he knew Julie was dead.

Bennet shook his head as he stood there, and said, 'I'm sorry.'

Harry asked him if his daughter had been mutilated.

'I'm sorry. She's burned,' replied Bennet tearfully.

Harry Christian then went upstairs to Julie's mum and broke the news. Pat screamed upon hearing it.

Ian Thomas became the prime suspect and was interviewed at length several times by the police. He seemed very cool and dispassionate, and only broke down once during questioning. Then he started to trip himself up during more police interviews. He said he had never been alone once since reporting Julie's disappearance, but the detectives who had taken down every statement from him and drawn up a large schematic floorchart detailing relevant information soon saw that Thomas had been alone for several periods. Each of these periods matched occasions when people in Teilo Street had reported the strange burning smell coming from the back alley. Thomas was arrested on the day the body was discovered.

A forensic scientist, Dr John Davidson, visited Julie's home and noticed that there were bathmats hanging over the banisters. They had been freshly washed and were still wet. The dressing-gown that Thomas claimed Julie had been wearing when he had last seen her was found washed. Davidson also noted that the whole house had quite recently been given a thorough spring-cleaning.

On 18 November Ian Thomas was charged with the murder of his common-law wife, and in Janury 1992 he was tried at Liverpool Crown Court for the murder of Julie Christian. At the beginning of the four-week trial Thomas denied murder and said he thought that Julie had been abducted or had even gone off with another man. But the cracks started to appear in Thomas's story when refuse collector Edgar Jackson was summoned by prosecuting counsel Rodney Klevan, QC, to pass on a curious but vital scrap of evidence. Jackson said that two days after Julie had vanished Thomas spoke to him at 11.15 a.m. Thomas had asked the binman if he had seen anything unusual in the alleyway behind his Teilo Street home on the previous day, as his girlfriend had been missing since Sunday. Jackson then said that Thomas told him that the police had found a bag and a shoe on a grassy area just over the road.

Prosecuting counsel Rodney Klevan then revealed to the jury that at 11.25 a.m., on wasteland known locally as the 'Diggers', a woman found a handbag which she took to Admiral Street Police Station. This woman returned to the same wasteland and found a shoe, which she took home before later calling the police. This shoe wasn't handed over to the police until 3 p.m. How, then, was Thomas able to reveal to Jackson that some of the victim's belongings had been found by police before they really had? Thomas had apparently made a gross error of timing.

Klevan told the court that the only person who needed to burn the body of Julie Christian was her boyfriend. If Julie had been murdered by a stranger, he went on, the killer would not have needed to obliterate the time and circumstances of her death. Klevan said, 'Why on earth, having killed her, would he want to stay there, make a fire and make sure it was alight and then return to it to help it along, to stoke it so it would continue to burn?'

Klevan drew attention to the fact that Thomas could not drive a vehicle, and so he dumped the corpse in the nearest logical place: the alley. He also got Thomas to admit that he had had a blazing row with Julie over an unpaid debt of £1,200 on the very day before she went missing.

A 10-year-old girl was called to give her account of an alleged sighting of Julie Christian that took place shortly after the time Thomas had last seen his common-law wife. Schoolgirl Emma Duffy said that her little brother Carl dropped his sweets in Teilo Street, and that Julie had picked them up. After speaking to Emma and Carl, she said goodbye and walked off towards High Park Street, which runs at right angles to the end of Teilo Street. Emma then told how she had spotted a stranger following Julie. According to the schoolgirl, Julie turned around to see the strange man, and reacted by walking faster, but then the man did the same. Julie raced around the corner at the end of the street and moments later the man did the same, and Emma never saw Julie again after that. When asked to describe the stranger, Emma said he had a blond, overgrown crewcut, and wore dark blue jeans and a sky blue ski jacket. This figure was never identified, and his presence, if we are to believe the schoolgirl's testimony, cannot be satisfactorily explained.

The defence counsel, Richard Henriques QC, told the jury, 'If Emma is correct then the prosecution case fails.'

On 10 February 1992 Ian James Thomas was convicted of murdering Julie Christian by a 10–2 majority, and was sentenced to life imprisonment by the judge, Mr Justice Waterhouse, who branded Thomas cold and callous. Waterhouse said to Thomas, who had remained impassive in the dock throughout the summing-up, 'You have rightly been found guilty by the jury. You behaved quite ruthlessly and callously in trying to save your own skin.'

Julie's family wept openly in the public gallery upon hearing the sentence.

On the day Ian Thomas began his life sentence, Harry Christian expressed his wish to know just how his daughter died so that he could begin to grieve properly. The cause of Julie's death was never determined, but

Home Office pathologist Dr James Burns had told the court that the only two possible causes of Julie's death were drowning or suffocation. One theory police considered was that Thomas had drowned Julie in the bathroom of their home before attempting to cremate her in the alley.

The stress of the murder left Harry unable to work, and forced him to undergo psychotherapy.

When Julie was laid to rest, her favourite book on the life of her hero, Paul McCartney, was buried with her.

16   Morphine and Matrimony

In 1904 a handsome young man named Robert Clements graduated from Queen's University in Belfast. He was a gifted conversationalist and had a charismatic aura about him. He specialized in gynaecology, but he was also a surgeon and physician, and he was also something of a Romeo. Clements had no shortage of young female admirers, but the good doctor married a plain-looking woman ten years his senior, and everybody suspected that Clements had only married the woman because she was the daughter of a wealthy miller. Two years after receiving £25,000 from her father in 1918, Clements' wife fell ill and later died, intestate. She had a mere £10 left in her savings, and before relatives of the dead woman could find out where the rest of Mrs Clements' fortune had disappeared to, Mr Clements took a trip across the Irish Sea and settled in Moss Side, Manchester, where he met and married a beautiful young colleen from County Antrim, who suspiciously died five years later. Dr Clements signed the death certificate himself and stated the cause of death as endocarditis, then put the £425 his second wife had left him into his bank account.

In 1928 Kathleen Burke succumbed to Clements' charm and became wife number three. After eleven years of marriage Kathleen died quite suddenly one day at their Southport home, and the widowed Dr Clements again benefited from the death of a spouse. Kathy left him £489 in her will. The police suspected that the death of this third wife was not a product of coincidence. They quickly telephoned the Liverpool Crematorium and gave the order to halt the incineration of Mrs Clements' body so that the corpse could be examined to see if it contained any traces of poison. But the call from the police came at the precise moment when Mrs Clements was being consumed by fire.

Undaunted by the police's suspicions, the audacious Dr Clements was soon seen walking hand in hand with the young porcelain-skinned Amy Victoria Barnett, the girl he had been seeing behind his late wife's back. Amy was the daughter of an immensely rich Lancashire magnate who wanted nothing but the best for his little girl, so he financed the grand wedding at St George's, in London's Hanover Square.

After the honeymoon the couple settled down in their luxurious, semi-detached Southport home. Mr and Mrs Clements were well liked by their neighbours and attended the nearby Christ Church without fail every Sunday morning. But married life turned sour for the Clements. Amy seemed to go cold, and on many occasions the doctor returned home to find that his carefree wife had not even bothered to cook him a meal.

When Mrs Clements died suddenly in May 1947, Dr J.M. Houston, the pathologist who performed the post-mortem, recorded the cause of death as myeloid leukaemia. The West Lancashire coroner was quick to act this time, and he despatched two detectives to cancel the funeral. Two Home Office forensic experts, Dr W.H. Grace and Dr J.B. Firth, were called in to examine the body of Mrs Clements. The doctors discovered that a kidney and several other organs were absent from the deceased woman. They had been removed by Dr Houston during the post-mortem and burned. So Dr Firth made a painstaking analysis of the remaining kidney and discovered one-third of a grain of morphine in it. He then carefully took several samples from the spinal column of the deceased and took them to his Preston laboratory. For a week Firth subjected the vertebrae samples to every known chemical screening process – and discovered one-twentieth of a grain of morphine. Amy Victoria Clement had been murdered.

Morphine crystals were also found in a hypodermic syringe belonging to Dr Clements, and the same drug was found in tablet form in a bottle labelled 'phenobarbitone'.

But the proof of murder came too late; Dr Clements was found dead at his home. A squirt of morphine from his syringe was the means of committing his *felo de se*.

It was a simple task for the jury to decide that the doctor had killed his last wife, but as the murderer had committed suicide there was no way of proving that the doctor killed his three previous wives, although it seems very likely that this was the case. If he did kill all of his wives, was it greed that drove the doctor to the despicable deeds? Or was he one who simply loathed the mind-numbing ennui of his marriages, and longed for a change of routine? This does seem to be the case, as shortly before his suicide, the doctor told a friend, 'I cannot remember when I ate a cooked meal in my own flat.'

17   Murder on the High Seas

It was in the month of April, 1857, when a gentle but
retarded seaman named Andrew Rose joined the crew of
the barque *Martha and Jane*, which was anchored off
Barbados. It didn't take Captain Henry Rogers long to
discover that the new member of his crew possessed a
slow-witted mind, and he and his fawning cronies,
William Miles (first mate) and Charles Seymour (second
mate), soon had it in for Rose.

Seymour gave Rose a simple task to perform on the
ship, but wasn't satisfied with the way the new recruit
set about his job, so he punched and kicked Rose until he
was black and blue. After that savage and gratuitous
beating, several members of the crew took pity on Rose
and urged him to run away; Rose took their advice. But
shortly afterwards he was captured by the police and
taken back to the *Martha and Jane* where he was put in
irons.

Now Captain Rogers had a real excuse to unleash his
brutal nature; and shortly after the barque set sail for
the port of Liverpool, Rose was mercilessly thrashed by
the captain and the first and second mates. They kicked
him and whipped him with a length of rope until they
were exhausted, leaving the poor halfwit's body a swollen
blood-soaked mess.

And the cruelty didn't stop there. Days later, the shackled Rose started singing a hymn when Captain Rogers appeared on deck. The captain instructed the first mate to fetch him a large iron bolt, which he then rammed into Rose's mouth. Miles and Seymour made sure the bolt, which was threatening to choke Rose, was kept securely in place by tying a strong length of yarn around Rose's head. Well pleased with their sport, the sadistic captain and his henchmen forced Rose to endure this ordeal for an hour-and-a-half before removing the bolt.

Another of the captain's perverted little pleasures was to set his dog on to Rose with the command 'Bite that man!' And the dog would charge at the unfortunate mariner and literally tear off chunks of his flesh. Many of the bite wounds sustained by Rose later became infected and ran with pus. But Rose's state of health didn't prevent the captain from sending him naked up the mast to furl the sail, with the first mate following behind with a whip. More sickeningly still, the captain would often make Rose eat his own excrement.

When the ship was a week out from Liverpool, Captain Rogers was standing on deck, surveying the pathetic sore-covered body of Andrew Rose when, with an expression of contempt on his weather-beaten face, he suddenly said: 'Rose, I wish you would either drown or hang yourself.'

Rose had endured enough, and did not care any more; he wanted to be rid of his terrible suffering, and he replied: 'I wish you would do it for me.'

Rogers reacted venomously to the mildly audacious act of insubordination; he and the two mates grabbed Rose by the arms and dragged him to the mainmast. A rope was produced and a noose was made. They put the noose over Rose's head and hanged him from the mainmast for two minutes. At the end of this time, Rose's eyes were bulging, and his protruding tongue was starting to turn black. The captain gave the order to release him, and Rose fell to the deck with a thump and lay there, inert. He was barely alive.

'If I'd kept him there just half a minute longer, he'd have been a goner!' Captain Rogers declared to his crew without a trace of compassion.

The terrifying ordeal proved too much for Rose, and shortly afterwards, on 5 June, after struggling up on to the deck in a semi-conscious state, he cried out, then died. The crew found the sight and stench of Rose's ulcerated and maggot-infested body unbearable. Captain Rogers ordered the festering corpse to be thrown into the sea.

Four days later the *Martha and Jane* arrived at Liverpool, and several members of the crew immediately reported Captain Rogers and his mates to the authorities. Rogers and his two partners in crime were taken into custody, and at St George's Hall on 19 August they were tried for the murder of Andrew Rose. The jury found them guilty, and when word of the verdict reached the huge mob assembled outside the building, Lime Street echoed to the sound of jubilant cheering.

Captain Henry Rogers, William Miles and Charles Edward Seymour were all sentenced to death, but the two mates were later reprieved.

The hitherto callous and brutal personality of Captain Rogers apparently underwent a dramatic change while he awaited execution in his cell at Kirkdale Gaol. He turned to God and prayed almost constantly through his final lonely days and nights.

On 12 September, at noon, the captain who had taken sadistic delight in torturing a simple-minded man and robbing him of his life, sampled some of the fear that Andrew Rose had felt under his wicked hand when he was taken to the scaffold in full view of a 30,000-strong crowd of laughing and jeering spectators. Until the white cap was pulled over his face by the hangman, Rogers stood on the gallows erected near the top of the prison wall and stared out at the sea's horizon, beyond the crowd below, beyond Liverpool Bay. The eternal sea was the last thing the captain saw. The sea that had been his life – and Andrew Rose's watery grave.

After the hanging a subscription was opened for the widow and five children of Captain Rogers, and £670 was collected – a substantial sum in those days.